David's Gift

SALLY THIBAULT

DAVID'S GIFT
First edition published in Australia 2010
This paperback edition published in United States 2012
Author: Sally Thibault
Website: www.davidsgift.com

Copyright © Sally Thibault 2009
Published by:
Wise Mothers Publishing
PO Box 1622, Oxenford
Queensland Australia 4209
www.wisemothers.com.au

National Library of Australia
Cataloguing-in-Publication entry:
Thibault, Sally
David's Gift – Asperger's Syndrome, Life & Love
One Family's Inspirational Journey from Diagnosis to Graduation

ISBN - 1453779930
ISBN - 13: 978-1453779934

Subjects:
1. Thibault, David
2. Parenting – Parenting of children with Autism
and Asperger's syndrome.
3. Dealing with ASD children in the school system.
4. Asperger's syndrome in Family Relationships.
5. Self actualization – Teaching parents how to
become the whole person/people they want
their children to become (Psychology).

Cover Design and Typesetting by:
P's in a Pod Creative
Chirn Park Queensland Australia
www.psinapod.com.au

For Gerry, David, Alissa, and Caitlin.

For the life we have and the love you give.

David's Gift

ASPERGER'S SYNDROME, LIFE & LOVE.
ONE FAMILY'S INSPIRATIONAL JOURNEY
FROM DIAGNOSIS TO GRADUATION

SALLY THIBAULT

WISE MOTHERS PUBLISHING – GOLD COAST – AUSTRALIA
WWW.DAVIDSGIFT.COM

TABLE OF CONTENTS

INTRODUCTION	IX
THE STORY	7
LEARNING TO LET GO	11
PATIENCE AND ACCEPTANCE	13
MILESTONES AND MEASURES	17
MY FIRST LESSON IN INTUITION	19
OUR SAD TIME	25
A NEW BEGINNING	27
OBSESSIONS—OUR NEW WORLD	31
GETTING LOST	33
SHOPPING	35
THOMAS THE TANK ENGINE	37
THERAPY	39
COMPUTERS—A WHOLE NEW WORLD	43
SCHOOL	45
THE ASSESSMENT AND THE REALITY CHECK	49
BULLYING—THE BEGINNING	51
SCHOOL DAYS	61
THE BULLYING INTENSIFIES	63
THE TURNING POINT	67
BEAN-BAG TIME	69
LIFE BECOMES MORE INTENSE	71
SPORT	77
TAE KWON DO—THE FIRST GREAT WIN	79
DISCOVERING THE DIAGNOSIS	85
NO, IT'S NOT BAD PARENTING!	89
THE MEDICATION JOURNEY	95
LEARNING MORE ABOUT ASPERGER'S SYNDROME	99
THE LIGHT BULB MOMENT	107
ALARM BELLS—TIME FOR CHANGE	113
ASCERTAINMENT TIME	119
HIGH SCHOOL	125
A NEW ERA, A NEW SET OF CHALLENGES	129
IT'S ALL ABOUT TO CHANGE	131

So the New Challenges Continue 133

Social Skills 141

Year 9—The Beginning of the End! 143

The Bullying Continues 151

Year 10—Crisis time 153

Crunch Time 155

A New Person Emerges, A New Family Evolves 159

A Place where Angels Live 161

My Boy Is Changing 165

Graduation 167

Onward and Upward 169

Girls and Relationships 173

My Special Moment 175

2010 177

David's Gift to Us as Parents 179

The Steps along the Way 185

The Four Steps to Authentic Fitness 187

Lessons Learned through Failure 197

Simplicity 201

Connecting with Nature 205

The Other Language 209

Making it all Work 211

Routines and Agreements 217

Creating Familiar Rituals 221

Our Journey 223

Just about Asperger's Syndrome 229

Inside Asperger's syndrome 231

A Swot Analysis of David 237

Food 241

Navigating Schools 243

Debriefing Time 245

Friends and Social Skills 247

Surviving Other Parents 249

It Takes a Village to Raise a Child 251

Those who Have Been There 253

About the Author 255

INTRODUCTION

Sometimes life hands you a challenge, that at the outset seems insurmountable, but later you realize was in fact a gift that changed your life.

This is our story.

From the time David was about two years old, we knew he was different from other children. He had an extremely limited vocabulary for his age. He found interaction with other people difficult, and any opportunity to play or relate with his peers often ended in an altercation or with tears. He bit other children for seemingly little reason and retaliated over the slightest thing with violence, and although a generally loving child at home, playing with other children was extremely challenging for him.

His sleep patterns were very erratic. We kept him busy during the day with various physical activities in an attempt to absorb some of his energy, and although he was often tired, he found getting to sleep at night difficult. We had a calming ritual every evening, which commenced with a bath, then dinner with candles and soft music playing, quiet time, and then in bed by 7:30 p.m., with either Gerry, my husband, or I reading to him. However, when it was my turn to read, after an hour or so, Gerry would often find me, book still in hand, asleep on David's bed while David was up wandering the house!

By the time he started school, the differences were more pronounced. He overreacted to certain stimuli, found it difficult to interact with his peers, and had little or no communication skills. From early on, we explored numerous medical and natural therapies, food allergy treatments, disciplines, educational programs, pills, and potions searching for the "something" that held the answer to the differences he faced, with most strategies having very little long-term success.

We actually came to believe at one time that it could be, as many people had often alluded to, our inability to discipline a strong-willed child and that a good swift smack on the behind was exactly what he needed!

After searching for answers for many years, in 1997, when David was twelve years old, he was finally diagnosed with Asperger's syndrome. Although today there are many medical professionals who understand this difference, in the 1990s, it was a different story.

Asperger's syndrome, sometimes called Autistic Spectrum Disorder (ASD), was first described in the 1940s by a Viennese pediatrician, Hans Asperger, and was recognized by the American Psychiatric Association in its *Diagnostic and Statistical Manual of Mental Disorders* for the first time when the fourth edition was published in 1994.

Asperger's syndrome is the term applied to the mildest and highest-functioning end of what is known as the autism spectrum. Those diagnosed with Asperger's syndrome find it difficult to understand social skills, often misunderstand the use of language in communication, and are usually considered "obsessive," focusing on one particular area of interest.

After David's diagnosis, we searched to find a "cure." Being very determined parents believing "you create your own reality," we embarked on a journey of discovery, exploring numerous treatments; medication, natural and physical therapies—you name it, we tried it. We were constantly testing new things and when one no longer worked, we would move to another brand new and improved strategy, pill, or therapy showing amazing results somewhere in the world.

During these times, our lives were overrun by emotions: anger, blame, frustration, sadness, and fear. I felt as if we were caught on a treadmill, constantly seeking solutions to find something that would make this word *Asperger's* go away.

Because the diagnosis and any knowledge of treatments or strategies to assist those with Asperger's syndrome was, at the time, very limited, I spent much of my free time trying to find out what caused this challenge in our family. I spent hours, weeks, and months looking for solutions from others, searching for the miracle cure that would make this "condition" go away, looking to blame somebody for this life we had been given.

I was angry. Very angry. This was not how our lives were supposed to be and I wanted it to be somebody's fault. I wanted somebody else to fix it and I wanted the world to know about it.

In the process, our lives began to spin out of control. We became trapped on a treadmill of blaming others, being angry with the world, trying to make the "system" (whatever that was) wrong. I wanted others to change; I wanted the world to change to suit my child. We ploughed head with a "victim" mentality and in the process lost our ability to trust our own intuition and judgments. A self-destructive cycle manifested in our lives, with poor business decisions leading to severe financial problems that affected our relationship and our health, and made our home a stressful place to be.

It wasn't until we reached breaking point that my husband, Gerry, and I made a decision: to take back the responsibility for our lives and for our child, to work on ourselves, to perceive who we were, and, in doing so, to explore the depths of our own emotions and beliefs.

David's Gift originally began as a book about Asperger's syndrome and the strategies we developed over the years that perhaps could help other families who are dealing with this diagnosis.

However, during the writing process, I came to realize how Asperger's syndrome had actually challenged and inspired us to comprehend who we really were and what it was we truly wanted out of life.

Dealing with David's Asperger's syndrome taught us the lessons we most needed to learn: the power of unconditional love, the value of patience and understanding, and the true meaning of the words *compassion, forgiveness, honesty,* and *authenticity.*

Those diagnosed with Asperger's syndrome are often intelligent, intense, and self-focused individuals who usually find success in a career requiring enormous amounts of attention to detail. But they view the world differently, and because of this "difference," they are often judged harshly as odd, over reactive, difficult, or noncompliant. For many, their brains and bodies are often over stimulated by things such as noise, light, heat, or cold. They can be overly sensitive to certain fabrics, smells, or odors, which causes them to react in ways deemed inappropriate.

Those with Asperger's often find relationships with others difficult to comprehend and miss the nonverbal cues that help people develop emotional depth and strong, interpersonal relationships. Through social interaction, we learn to experience love, patience, compassion, and understanding as well as all the emotions that make up the fabric of who we are. For those with Asperger's, these experiences and emotions often don't come naturally and have to be learned, usually only through modeling other's behaviors. How to act in certain situations or how to self-monitor stress or confusion can be challenging because in their world, they do not need social acceptance, and so do not grasp others reactions. Hence, they don't naturally comprehend what is and is not acceptable behavior. If it doesn't feel OK, then they will react in whatever way they feel necessary in order to cope with the stress of the situation at hand.

Being able to deal effectively with the many challenging and confusing aspects of David's diagnosis meant that we, as his parents, had to be in tune with his needs. We needed to be constantly aware of how we interacted, not only with David but also with each other, with our daughters, and with the people we associated with on a daily basis.

It was our role to become the people we wanted David to be.

We needed to ensure that our emotions were clear and real so David could learn to decipher his own emotions and exhibit unconditional love, patience, and compassion, so he could "feel" what they were and understand them in his life.

We had to be clear in our communication, use language that was positive and succinct, and be very, very sure that what we said was exactly what we both wanted and intended.

It has been an amazing journey.

The story you are about to read is the story of our family. There are many moments of joy and any moments of love and laughter. However, there are also many sad moments and many dark moments, some of which were very difficult to write; but I felt it important to share the darkest times because through those times our greatest lessons were learned.

When Asperger's syndrome first came into our lives, it presented to us a challenge that, at the time, seemed sad, unfair, and overwhelming. It is only now I can see it was in fact an incredible gift. Because, you see, the things we most needed to teach David were the things we most needed to learn ourselves.

This was the gift David gave us, a gift for which we will forever be grateful.

THE STORY

There is something about the birth of the first grandchild in a family.

It is a special time filled with hopes and great anticipation: the prospective grandmother wanting to know about the first flutter; daughter and mother sharing the symptoms only a first time mother could possibly feel; a protective and proud grandfather steering conversations at the local golf club to due dates and weight gains; and an exceptionally proud and perhaps a little fearful first-time Dad suddenly entering a world of incredible excitement and tremendous responsibility, all at the same time.

For siblings of the first-time parents, the prospect of the first niece or nephew is greeted with conversations revolving around the newest strollers, natural fibers, discussions about the perfect doctor, the perfect birthing option, with younger sisters and brothers eagerly awaiting the joy of being an uncle and an aunt.

Books are widely read; decisions are made about the incredibly important delivery procedure; ultrasound photos sent to grandparents and shared at coffee mornings and workplaces with associates feigning some degree of interest in said photos as they peer to find the correct appendage to discover whether it's a boy or girl, the one who will change the world.

We were older parents: Gerry was thirty-eight, and I, twenty-eight. We had waited a while to have a baby. We met in Canada in 1979, lived together for a while, created a business from scratch, came home to Australia, got married, went back to build an even bigger business, then in the midst of its success opted for "sea change," we just didn't know it was called that at the time. We relocated from a minus-30-degree-Celsius winter in Edmonton, Alberta, to an incredibly hot, humid plus-30-degree-Celsius summer in Queensland, Australia.

David was conceived in 1984, after many months of trying and suggestions that I needed to stop exercising as intensely as I was and concentrate on the process of conception.

It worked. In mid-October 1984, I advised Gerry and whoever else passed me in the street, spoke to me on the phone, or stood next to me in the line at the bank that I was, in fact, expecting a baby!

We were "new age" parents, on the lookout for natural childbirth. I had read a book on water births and made the decision that this was for me.

It was not a normal practice in 1985, let alone now, so the search for a midwife and a water birthing center led to a clinic in Melbourne and to Dr. Bruce and his wife, June. It was perfect; we had found the perfect solution to the medical intervention of modern science.

We, the older parents of a new baby, armed with way too much knowledge and information, decided our baby would be born in the water, with music and candles. Our baby was going to be different!

I had predicted that he would be born at the end of May, and I made the decision to move home to my parents' place for the last few weeks and Gerry would fly down on weekends to await the birth of this beautiful baby who would gracefully enter the world when we were ready and the time was perfect.

LEARNING TO LET GO

My first lesson in learning to let go in this brave new world of parenthood was during the final weeks before David was born.

As much as I wanted this birth to go the way I had planned, our baby had other ideas. Over a series of three weekends, Gerry flew to Melbourne, where we sat and waited and talked to our baby, intellectually and spiritually connecting with this child, cajoling this little human creature to please make the grand entrance on this weekend so Daddy can be there.

Finally, two weeks past my due date, Dr. Bruce delivered the news. It was time for induction; this little one was a little too comfortable and needed a little assistance in entering the new world. So, with the beautiful suitcase packed, complete with birth music and candles, I was admitted to Queen Victoria Hospital, Florence Nightingale Ward, where the process of enticing this baby into the world began.

Patience and Acceptance

My second lesson in parenting was just around the corner. After commencing the induction, Dr. Bruce suggested walking would help speed up the process of birth, so following the procedure, that morning I refused breakfast, waited for Gerry to arrive and we commenced walking along the wards of the Queen Victoria Hospital—new parents eager and glowing with the knowledge that within hours, we would be parents.

Hours and hours and hours! Short breaks for a light snack and again the walking would start again, intermittent labor pains signaling that we were on our way.

However, as the hours wore on and the pain became worse, Gerry was concerned about me. Finally, after ten hours, he convinced me to lie down and wait for the doctor to arrive. Hearing "Two centimeters dilated; I will see you in the morning" brought tears of pain and tiredness. I pleaded with the doctor. "I have a pretty high threshold of pain, but I don't think I can take much more." And with the curtains closed, I heard him say to the nurse, "Nil by mouth. I think we need to move to the birthing unit." Not realizing "nil by mouth" meant that the doctor was expecting that I would be undergoing a caesarean section; I was just so pleased that we would finally be on the move to the real, live place where babies were born.

The hours wore on and we walked more; the pains by this stage were debilitating. Finally, the midwife convinced me an epidural would help. It was the one thing I didn't want…where was the natural birth? I had seen it before on all those soap operas: mother-to-be with perfect makeup, sucking on ice and breathing, panting and whooshing; and after a few pushes, out comes a beautiful soft pink baby; and she cries and kisses her gorgeous husband; and the music plays. Hang on—I have no makeup, I am crying, I have just thrown up, and I look a mess, and *now* you want to give me an epidural?

Oh, but what relief! Now I will be able to push out our beautiful baby. I think I fell asleep, I can't remember really, but the next thing I knew, Gerry was holding my hand and the midwife saying, "We can't wait. Your baby is getting distressed. I have called Dr. Bruce and we are going to do an emergency caesarean." A thirty-two-hour labor was taking its toll not only on our gorgeous baby, but on me as well.

The feeling of failure was overwhelming, but so was the exhaustion. OK, I've had enough; I am not good at this birthing process let's get this over with.

I didn't realize at the time, but for Gerry, this experience was his worst nightmare. His mother had died in childbirth while giving birth to his brother who was four years younger than him. So not only the reality and the emotion of losing a mother but also his understanding what his father had gone through in losing a wife was something he remembered vividly. So during this process, he was also going through a great deal of distress because he felt so helpless and out of control, and nothing he could do, or say, could fix it.

At 4:10 am on Thursday, June 6, 1985, our beautiful nine-pound, nine-ounce baby boy was born in the operating theatre of the Queen Victoria Hospital. And my goodness he was beautiful. "The most beautiful baby in the nursery," said the nurse, and I, of course, knew that!

With olive skin like his dad and with deep brown, almost black, eyes that seemed to allow you to peer right into his soul, he looked just like me when I had been a baby, and he slept and slept. It had been a rough entry into the world.

Proud, proud grandparents arrived within hours. The newly made Nana, crying and looking like she had been awake all night (and of course, she had), and proud Papa holding his first grandchild as we proudly introduced David Calvin Thibault; Calvin, my father's name, had been in the family for generations.

We had so many goals and plans and dreams for this amazingly beautiful baby boy.

After the trauma of the very eventful labor and emergency caesarean, David's first few weeks in the world were blissful.

He and I took to breastfeeding like old-timers. He slept in our room and delighted in being around us. He was alert, inquisitive, joyful, and playful. He especially loved his bath time; watching the trees blowing in the wind; music and dancing with me.

Having been a fitness instructor for many years, I created a fitness routine, using him as a weight, as I tentatively started to do some sit-ups and bench presses—I would hold him in a great big bear hug as I lifted my shoulders off the ground, each time giving him a big kiss on the cheek. He would squeal with delight with an enormous smile each time one of the kisses landed on his cheek.

We had a wonderful routine. I'm a Virgo and a firstborn child, so routines are bliss! We would be up early for feeding; would spend time with Gerry for breakfast before he left for work; then do a load of washing, clean up the kitchen, and perhaps a small nap before getting dressed and heading off to a Nursing Mothers meeting somewhere.

Having always worked, I had a network that revolved around people I worked with. Now, at home for the first time, I had the desire and need to make a new network of friends to led me to the fabulous, accepting women of the Nursing Mothers Association. They helped, gave advice, and were generally very accepting and ever patient with this new mum who wanted to know everything.

On return home, a feed and a nap for mum and baby, before once again putting David back into the stroller and heading off for a six-kilometer walk every day. It was a routine often interrupted by people stopping to comment about how beautiful he was, and David, with his big brown eyes and enormous toothless smile, would respond to people. He enjoyed the attention and put on a show every time.

MILESTONES AND MEASURES

Did I mention we not only had the best-looking baby, but the smartest? Oh, OK then, we did.

We read to David in utero, and we continued reading the same books from birth. I bought books with textures so he could feel and touch the words and pictures, and a favorite pastime of his was sitting on the couch with Gerry reading the Saturday papers!

For our first Christmas, we flew to Melbourne to be with Nana, Papa, Uncle Martin, and all the aunties. It was a joyful Christmas.

David delighted in the attention from the aunties and from his uncle, who fussed over him and took it in turns playing with him or taking him for a walk. He adored Cleo, our much cherished Labrador/Kelpie-cross dog, which I had bought for a dollar at a school fete many years before and who had quickly become a member of our large family. Cleo enjoyed all the attention she received from David, sitting patiently while he patted her or rather pulled her fur and ears!

But most of all he loved Nana and Papa, who, as first time grandparents doted on him.

His favorite game was to play peek-a-boo with Daddy and Uncle Martin. With a great toothless grin and perched high on

Daddy's shoulders, he would squeal with delight when Uncle Martin would hide behind the door then pop out and say boo.

The best part of Christmas was when Nana put him among the big pile of discarded Christmas wrappings in the middle of the living room floor and he could just play happily, making noise with it and the tasting all of it.

We had such fun on that holiday; enjoying bush walks, and visits with friends who had also just become parents. David relished the attention and the socializing. He was so alert and funny and enjoyed being around people. It was a perfect holiday.

Soon, however, things changed.

MY FIRST LESSON IN INTUITION

Next stop, immunizations.

Now, I am not sure why I had this feeling of dread every time somebody mentioned immunization, but this sick feeling would come over me. At mothers' meetings, at the gym at coffee mornings, and at play mornings, new mothers discussed immunizations and how dreadful were those parents who didn't immunize their children.

I was in two minds. Yes, I thought, I must be the good mother and immunize my child. I would be very irresponsible if I didn't, but something was nagging at me—a fear, a dread, a dark thought about it not being right for my child. I couldn't put my finger on it. I didn't discuss it with anybody. I just avoided it as long as I could so somehow I could delay the process.

In January of 1986, a number of children who spent time in the daycare room at the health club where I worked were sick, and an outbreak of whooping cough was being reported in the papers. I felt I must, as a responsible parent, do the right thing and listen to those that knew better than I did. So I booked the appointment for David's first round of immunizations.

Diphtheria, tetanus, and whooping cough; the cocktail of three immunizations entered my son's body in the morning, with the usual precautionary warning from the doctor to watch for any unexpected rises in temperature and, if concerned, to give him a dose of child's pain and fever medication.

That day I watched him closely. His arm was a little swollen and red, but nothing out of the ordinary, other than he appeared a little listless.

That night David didn't feed well. He was fitful and hot, so I gave him some medication as suggested by the doctor. He slept through the night, but not comfortably, and he groaned when I moved him. I put it down to a sore arm and pulled him into bed with us, allowing him to feed when he wanted.

By nine the next morning, he was not well at all. He would only feed in small bursts, then would pull his legs up to his chest and cry as if waiting for a pain to subside, and then vomit before finally lying back, flat on the bed and exhausted.

By 10am his crying was getting worse and he was turning gray. I phoned the doctor and was told to bring him in straight away. As soon as I arrived at the surgery, the nurse took me straight in to his office.

The doctor took one look at him and advised me to admit him to hospital immediately as he was becoming dehydrated. He thought David may have contracted gastroenteritis, which was spreading throughout our area at the time. I had called Gerry before I left for the doctors, so he met us there and we rushed our little one to the hospital. Our doctor phoned ahead to advise we were on our way.

The wonderful young doctors and nurses were at the door to meet us. They admitted David straight to the pediatric ward and immediately inserted a drip, although because by now he was very dehydrated, the process took a few attempts.

David was taken into an isolation ward, and now, with fluid entering his body, he slept until, fitfully, and he would pull his knees up to his chest and throw up again.

The night was long, with little sleep.

Next morning, I woke early to his cries. Once again, his knees were up to his chest, and I gently opened his diaper to find a red jelly substance. Luckily, the nurses' station was right next to the bed. I pushed on the buzzer and the nurse took one look at David and left to get the doctor.

The next five minutes were like a scene from a medical emergency show. Nurses and doctors arrived from nowhere and while the nurses started to wheel David out of the isolation ward, doctor tried to explain what the problem was.

"Bowel intussusceptions occur when one portion of the bowel slides into the next. When this occurs, it creates an obstruction in the bowel, with the walls of the intestines pressing against one another. We have two options. We have to get him to theater immediately. We will endeavor to have the bowel right itself with a barium enema; if that fails, we will have to operate. Call your husband now; we need to get underway immediately, and we need you to sign the consent form."

Oh my God, this can't be happening.

An urgent call to Gerry, days prior to mobile phones, and the next thing I was being fitted with a heavy protective vest and watching my tiny baby in an X-ray room. The tube was inserted, and we watched as the bowel moved itself, righting the wrong.

Within minutes, my seriously ill baby was resting comfortably and desperate for a feed. By the time Gerry arrived, it was all over. I think we both aged about ten years that morning.

All fixed, all wonderful again. Back home again to anxious phone calls from grandparents, aunties, uncle, and friends. A miraculous recovery.

"Children are amazing," my mother said "Just when you think the worst, they sit up and smile." Man, I was exhausted.

But something changed; little things, not outstanding by any means, but small things.

David became quieter, more introspective. The gains he had made in the months prior seemed to slow a little, not a lot, just a little. He would watch a show on TV and now, instead of pulling himself up to the TV to try to interact with the figures on the screen, he sat and watched, as if curious about what the figures on the screen were actually doing there!

He was more withdrawn when around children he didn't know. Children he knew were fine, and he played with friends' older children, but there was a difference. It seemed to take him longer to grasp things, taking longer to master the art of banging on the drum or playing with the toy tool set, and he became obsessive about certain toys and books.

Crawling wasn't part of the milestones however. One minute he was lying; the next, he was sitting; and at nine months old, he pulled himself up and started walking.

Being a first-time parent, I didn't see any problem with missing that essential milestone. I just thought he was exceptionally bright and clever; however many years and many hours of occupational therapy later, I realized how crucial this was to so many issues that arose in David's development.

He had little hand–eye coordination. We would roll the ball to him, but he couldn't seem to judge putting his arms out to receive the ball and then roll it back, like other children.

Well into his second year, David still wasn't talking.

He had standard words—*dad, mom, no*—but his vocabulary didn't evolve. He would point to things. "You give into him too easily," said the pediatrician. "When he points to things, make him say the word, repeat it back." So began the arduous process of trying to coax David to speak. If he pointed to something, we would say, "Would you like an apple David? Say *apple*," which he usually didn't.

Towards the end of 1986, I had returned to full-time teaching. Fortunately, the gym where I taught fitness classes had a child-minding facility, and David was able to come with me each day.

David loved the gym and being around the other children, but the differences in him were starting to show, especially when he was trying to interact with other children. "David seems happier playing on his own," said the day care assistant, "and becomes rather obsessive about the toys he wants. Sometimes, this results in him hitting others to get what he wants." This led to, what became the repetitive "David, when you want a toy, you mustn't hit other children. Just ask nicely, 'Can I please play with that?' Or 'Can I have a turn now?'" It was the same phrases every day. Sometimes it worked. Most times it didn't.

Just before David turned two, I fell pregnant again.

We had planned to have another child and it seemed no sooner had we decided this, that a pregnancy test I took showed a positive result.

When I was six months' pregnant, Gerry and I both felt that David would benefit from three days in full-time day care, and I needed a break. He needed to learn to socialize with children, and perhaps his extra energy was a lack of stimulation throughout the day. Besides, when this next baby was born, I wanted to be able to spend quality time with him or her, without worrying which fence David was climbing or whether he had pulled the chair over to the door, unlocked it, and was now riding his tricycle in the middle of the road—a common occurrence!

At the time, day care centers were few and far between. I visited a number of centers fairly close to our house however most of these were booked and had waiting lists. A friend told me about one being built, about twenty minutes from where we lived and in the opposite direction to work, but I jumped in the car quickly and headed down to put David's name on the list.

Scallywags—a modern, beautiful day care center—was sunny, clean, and had a huge outside playing area enormous sand pit. David was in seventh heaven.

David's carer, Donna, happened to be doing a university degree part-time and was about to begin an assignment on gifted and talented children. When I arrived to pick David up from his very first day in his new "school," she spoke to me.

"I think David would fall under the gifted and talented spectrum. He has an amazing memory, is very alert, and knows his colors and numbers," she said.

"But he's not talking yet," was my response.

"That can be normal in gifted children, but why don't you go and see Community Health and look into him seeing a speech therapist. In the meantime, I would like to spend time observing David for my assignment, if you don't mind."

Mind? Of course not, spend as much time as you want observing my genius child!

Our Sad Time

In August 1987, my mother lost her long and very painful battle with cancer. It was devastating for all of us. She had been such a strong part of our family, and I had especially enjoyed the relationship we had developed since David was born.

Mum was the most amazingly patient person in the world. She loved David and he loved her. During the last few visits however, it became more difficult for her to spend time with David because, as she said, he was "very boisterous!"

Mum loved taking him for a walk, but because of his unpredictability, she would use a child restraint, as the cancer made it harder for her to move quickly. She read to him, played with him, and seemed to have that incredible sixth sense when it came to understanding him.

Two years earlier, Mum had been diagnosed with breast cancer, and after a mastectomy and subsequent chemotherapy treatment, she appeared to have won the fight. Six months later, however, cancer was detected in her hip, which pressed upon her sciatic nerve, which made moving very painful. She fought a valiant battle, switching her diet to organic foods, seeking solace in meditation, and resigning from her job in order to battle the disease. In July 1987, it became obvious her fight was drawing to a close, and Dad and Mum made the long and very slow journey from Melbourne to Queensland. She had grown up in Queensland, and my father knew that she wanted to spend her last few weeks with her family surrounding her. She and Dad rented a house on the beach on the southern end of the Gold Coast. Two of her sisters, who were nurses, were able to care for her in her last few days, fulfilling her desire not to die in a hospital, and on August 5 at 10 a.m., she passed away, surrounded by her husband, her children, and their partners.

It was so sad to realize David was the only grandchild she would know. She would have been the most wonderful Nana to all of her eleven grandchildren. A terrible sadness enveloped all of us—my father, my three sisters and my brother, and our partners.

Some things in life are just so terribly unfair and sad. Losing my mother when she was only fifty-five years old, having recently retired and was so looking forward to enjoying life, was one of those times.

A NEW BEGINNING

Despite our sadness and loss, my second pregnancy was a beautiful experience again. I taught fitness classes right up until a week before Alissa was born, stopping only because the men in my classes stopped coming because they were so worried I was going to have the baby right there and then in the middle of the class!

Dad moved in with us for a few months, and he was very much looking forward to the birth of this new grandchild, a new beginning for all of us.

Dr. Ivan was the gentle doctor we had chosen for this blessed birth of our daughter. "I would like to try for a natural birth," I said, convinced that the first difficult birth was only because David was the size he was. "No problem," said Dr. Ivan. "The choice is yours; however, I would suggest we revisit the situation a couple of weeks before she is due and then make our decision."

Our decision?

For a long time after David's birth, I had felt an extreme sense of failure because I had required a caesarean section when he was born. After his birth, I would often come across people (mostly other women) who, after giving birth naturally, would raise an eyebrow in judgment after hearing my story, as if, by some twist of nature, children who are born naturally were somehow superior or better than children who are born by caesarean.

So those feelings of failure and of being out of control were now compounded by my feeling rather helpless with the whole toddler-raising thing. I had received another call from the day care center to say David had bit another child again. I was starting to believe perhaps I was a dreadful mother who was not only a failure at the whole birthing thing but also was obviously not disciplining her son properly.

So by Dr. Ivan giving me the opportunity to make the decision, I felt, for a moment, empowered, although in the end, again, a caesarean section was my only option. This time, however, I felt more in control and more powerful, knowing that the choice was made because of a physical issue.

On a very warm January day in 1988, our little redheaded daughter arrived into the world. David and Gerry both were decidedly over the moon at the entrance of another female into the family.

David took a liking to his baby sister immediately, and she responded, absolutely delighted in having a brother who wanted to know where she was and what she was doing every minute of the day. However, I would have to watch him all the time. If she was asleep, he would just climb into the bassinet to see if she was breathing and would try opening her eyes to wake her up, prompting me to remove the bassinet from its stand and place it on the floor.

I was worried for years that Alissa would develop one arm or leg longer than the other as, being too heavy for him to lift, David felt the best way to get his new baby sister from one place to the next was to grab either a wrist or an ankle and pull. He would look at me quite indignantly as I yelled, "David, stop!" A pained look would cross his face—he just wanted to play with her!

Our lives revolved around routine. Speech Therapy for David was one of those routines. Each fortnight we paid a visit to the speech therapist with scrapbook in hand and a new lot of exercises to try. By four, David was still not speaking fluently, although words such as *mum, dad, papa, puppy, Lisslus* (Alissa's new nickname) were used often.

David became obsessed in all things *Spot. Spot* books were read over and over again. *Spot,* the TV show, and *Spot* videos were watched continuously. Then one day he found another book, sort of like *Spot*, because it had flaps that lifted when you had to find the animals the story related to, and *Dear Zoo* became a favorite book of his for many months. He memorized every word and every picture. The book had to be read at the same speed and with the same expressions and intonation each time. If not, we had to start all over again. Sometimes, I would, in my tiredness or boredom, try to skip parts, but it would never work; we would have to start all over again.

At this point, I was sure David was actually reading. He knew all the words and could recognize them, hence my belief that he was, in fact, chronologically ahead of other children in his reading level. I didn't realize at the time that he memorizing the words.

David had a photographic memory for words that interested him, but he had absolutely no idea how to then take those words and use them in other contexts, which, of course, is the basis by which we learn language. He was like a child who had arrived on the planet with no innate, intuitive understanding of language. But this was something I didn't realize until many years later. For now, we thought he was a genius!

OBSESSIONS—OUR NEW WORLD

Slowly and surreptitiously, routines and obsessions became part of our lives. At first, I just thought it was a normal part of growing up. It seemed that many of our friends also went through the same thing with their children. It's just that in our house, David became obsessive about certain things that if not adhered to, resulted in hours of inconsolable distress.

Each time a new obsession would commence, it would start with a seemingly innocent beginning. In order to try to get David involved, to encourage conversation, and to begin to identify different colors, when we were in the car, I began talking to him about the traffic lights. "Look, David, it's a red light. Wait; here comes the yellow light, and what happens when it goes green?" "Go!" would be his excited call from the backseat.

Traffic lights then became an obsession. He loved them. When we went on walks, he wanted to stand and watch the traffic lights go from green to yellow to red and then back again. When we would come up to his favorite intersection, which had no less than four sets of traffic lights that all changed colors at different times to allow cars to turn in different directions, he would start to bounce up and down in his seat squealing in delight. "Oh! Oh! Red, nearly go, yellow...green means go;

green means go"—until I responded, "That's right David. Green means go!"

The other obsession developed again around color. Our local shopping center had colored signs in the parking lot identifying the different parking lanes—lane number four was a green sign, number six was a red sign, and number seven was a brown sign.

I am not sure how this particular obsession started, but for some reason, every time we went to this particular shopping center, we had to park in "brown seven." If David knew we were going shopping, from the time we left the house, he would say, "Brown seven, park in brown seven," over and over again. If I tried to deviate and park in "red six," he would obsessively chant, "No, park in brown seven, brown seven...park." I remember one particular day waiting for ten minutes before a space became available in brown seven; I couldn't deal with the obsessive questioning if we parked somewhere else! It was as if brown seven had become the safe space. He knew how long it took to get from a particular parking area to the front door of the mall and how many steps it took to get from the doors to the car again. He obsessed with the color brown and the number seven, often commenting when he saw the word *seven* written that "this one is not brown seven. Brown seven is not here. It is in the parking lot."

When we would count to ten with different objects or things, he would often then stop at the number seven and say, "But this is not brown seven, this is a different seven." He repeated the statement until I responded, "That's right, David; this is not brown seven. This is a different seven."

GETTING LOST

Toward the end of 1988, Gerry was awarded one of the top sales awards at the real estate office where he worked. So in the October of that year, we headed off to Canada, to introduce David and Alissa to our friends, Ted and Judy, who we had known since the early eighties. We couldn't wait to introduce them to our new family.

At first, we had reservations about taking David and a ten-month-old baby on a seventeen-hour plane trip, but they both traveled like seasoned travelers. We bought David a talking, toy computer and a portable personal tape player with headphones (a long time before iPods!). He was totally enthralled with them; the computer and the tape player, together with the fact we were traveling on an airplane, resulted in a very excited three-and-a-half-year-old being more than happy to stay in his seat, a fact which had amazed both of us.

David loved Canada, mostly because the cars in Canada drove on the other side of the road, but even better than that, the traffic lights were different. They hung from wires in the center of the road. He thought that was amazing.

Ted and Judy had a small dog (poodle-muddle, as Ted called her) called Sheena. David loved her, and she took to David as though they had known each other for years.

One afternoon, while we were all having coffee, I suddenly realized it was very quiet. A quick check of the apartment, the pool, and the park adjacent to the unit confirmed that David had gone missing. For the next twenty minutes, we panicked—searching the park, the playground, and the apartment complex. My heart was racing; Judy and Ted prepared to start knocking on the doors of the other apartments in the complex.

Then it dawned on me: the traffic lights!

We left Alissa with Ted and Judy, and Gerry and I ran the two blocks to the main road, and sure enough, there was David standing at the curb, watching the traffic lights, with Sheena dutifully sitting right next to him.

As we got to him, I didn't know whether to yell at him or hug him. My first question was, *"David, what on earth are you doing?"* He didn't take his eyes off the lights and said, *"Watching the traffic lights ... oh, oh, red, now green."*

"David, you could have gotten lost. You are only three and a half years old. You can't be walking up here on your own!" He was not fazed one little bit, and even when we were walking home, his hand firmly in mind, and his eyes were still fixed on the traffic lights behind him.

Many years later, we were talking to David about Canada and I asked him if he remembered when he walked up to watch the traffic lights by himself. *"Oh yes,"* he said. *"I remember that. But I wasn't by myself. I took Sheena with me so she would help me get home again."*

There were so many similar incidents throughout David's life. His reasoning for what he did and why he did it very often didn't match his age, his ability to communicate, or in fact make sense to anybody else. However, once we began to understand how he thought and how he reasoned, it helped us to come to terms with so many different situations throughout his life. At the same time, it made parenting David a little like riding a roller-coaster—we never quite knew what was around the next corner.

SHOPPING

Shopping with David was a game of cat and mouse and was another example of his very different reasoning. David, meanwhile, thought I was really quite strange in my demands that he wait until I was ready to take him to wherever he wanted to go. In his mind, it was a perfectly reasonable thing to do—to be four years old and do exactly what he wanted, when he wanted. I had to keep my eyes on him all the time and give him something to do so he wouldn't wander off. In our family, a simple shopping trip meant lots of lateral thinking and being one step ahead of David's thought processes all the time.

Each shopping expedition would start the same way. First, as I got Alissa out of the car, I would make David hold the stroller so "it doesn't roll away," or, rather, he didn't wander away. I would then give him jobs to do while we were in the super-market: pick out the best apples, find the milk, and make sure the items went in the shopping cart in a neat way (like when he played with Lego blocks). I would talk about where eggs came from or how milk was made, anything to keep his mind focused on staying where I could see him.

However, if I stopped to look at an item for too long, or if I became engaged in a conversation with other people, David would invariably wander off.

Whilst the thought of a four-year-old child being alone in a shopping center was very scary for me— David had no fear or concern about it at all. He had other things to do, and besides, he would be in one of two places: the toilet or the bookshop. And sure enough, after first checking the toilets (or asking a kind gentleman to do it for me), I would find David in one of the bookshops, sitting on the floor, down the end of the aisle, reading a Spot book or later on a Thomas the Tank Engine book, which became the obsession after Spot finally wore off.

It was all very predictable really. It's just my heart would beat so fast, and all the awful thoughts about him being taken by strangers would often cloud any reasonable judgments. I spent many a shopping trip abandoning a half-filled shopping cart, hauling Alissa out of the baby seat, and rushing from the supermarket in search of David, just in case one day he didn't do what I thought he would do.

THOMAS THE
TANK ENGINE

At the same time as Spot, we were introduced to the world of Thomas the Tank Engine—a vignette that appeared for five minutes before the only TV shows I would let the children watch: a children's show called *Play School*, followed by *Babar* or *Madeline*, animated shows based on the famous children's books.

Thomas the Tank Engine came on at 3:55 p.m. every day, followed by *Play School* at 4. Now I am not sure when it became an obsession, but I realized one afternoon that I was panicking because I didn't think we would make it home by 3:50. Palms sweating, heart beating, I wondered what would we do if we missed Thomas? I didn't have to wait long to find out—we missed it, which then resulted in hours of "Thomas? Thomas? No Thomas today?" — an obsessive mantra that carried on throughout the night.

We bought a video recorder to solve the issue. Within a few hours of our buying it, David had mastered how to record tapes, rewind, fast-forward, and set the timer so we could tape Thomas—all before I had even taken the instruction booklet out of the plastic envelope.

Unfortunately, however, it didn't really solve the issue. To record *Thomas the Tank Engine* and to watch Thomas at exactly 3:55 every afternoon was not the same thing.

Even though I would reassure him that the VCR would record the show, he was actually seeking the routine of watching the show at 3:55. If we were out of the house at that time, his routine was upset. The obsession and the routine had a number of aspects; all involved him feeling safe and secure and helped him to create order in his world, a lesson I learned much later.

THERAPY

"David has not developed his fine or gross motor skills and is significantly behind the other children of his age. Have you considered occupational therapy?"

At this stage in David's life, we were still dealing with numerous physical and emotional issues, which seemed to increase as he got older, and he became more and more separated from his peers in his stages of development.

I began to really question where on earth this had all gone so wrong. What had happened to take this incredibly advanced, interactive child in those early months, to a child who was constantly challenged with so many issues?

I started doubting my ability as a parent. I read the books; I played the games; I spent hours breastfeeding, hugging, playing peek-a-boo. We sang, we played, we talked to people, and we spent time socializing with children his age. Why was it we had to deal with so many seemingly simple challenges? Was it because we were older parents and less easygoing? Was it because we didn't discipline enough or disciplined too much? Why was it that people had stopped asking us over for play dates?

I knew in my heart that he really didn't mean it when he hit other kids or bit the hand of the person who wanted to take away the toy he loved. Were we doing something that was making our child obsessive?

In my mind, I began to rationalize different options. Perhaps many of these behaviors were occurring because although he was intellectually advanced, he was physically and verbally behind his peers and behind what was age appropriate, and this was creating frustration for him. The frustration then manifested and he lashed out at other children.

One day I spoke to our speech therapist, and she suggested that perhaps occupational therapy could help with his coordination. So for the next two years, visiting the occupational therapist became another regular therapy.

The occupational therapist, like the speech therapist, became like a close friend. Between sounds, words, colors, and pictures, we practiced crawling, climbing through hoops, and, the best of all, swinging in an enclosed swing that hung from the ceiling, David's favorite thing.

"It's probably because he didn't crawl. He is very bright and remembers everything, but crawling is such an integral part of life; he has missed these important developmental milestones…"

David loved water but hated swimming lessons, although we persisted with those from the time he was eighteen months old. So to help develop his hand–eye coordination and his spatial awareness, the occupational therapist suggested that we purchase a small boogie board to work with at home in the pool. The "game" (i.e., therapy) involved him lying flat on his tummy on the board and I then had to push the board across the pool. The actions of kicking and paddling, knowing when to stop, turning himself around, and kicking off the wall to get back to me were all designed to increase not only his physical strength but also his sense of space in relation to other objects and people around him.

For six months, we spent every day in the water patiently playing the many games designed to help David improve his coordination. David loved being in the pool and saw the time we spent together as great fun. His confidence, his spatial awareness, and his ability to swim improved greatly.

We also had a great deal of fun being in the pool together every afternoon. Alissa was always in the pool with us and would swim around, pretending to be a dolphin, or would grab her own boogie board and have me do the same exercises for her as well. Both Alissa's and David's abilities in the water improved greatly, and they both became very proficient swimmers as a result. I have often thought back to that time and have realized how much improvement in their swimming abilities came from half an hour of fun in the pool every afternoon.

However, although we began to see some improvements in David's physical coordination, his language was still very limited and the obsessive behaviors began to get more pronounced as he got older. Something wasn't right, but no matter how many experts we saw or how many tests David endured, there was no definitive answer, other than perhaps we didn't discipline him enough!

COMPUTERS—A
WHOLE NEW WORLD

A t the beginning of 1989, we bought our first computer. David was fascinated. Gerry only had to tell him once how to load a game and David would spend hours (if we let him) playing games and figuring out the intricate nature of how those little images fell down the screen in the very first computer game installed on the computer, called Bubble Bubble.

Alissa loved playing on the computer as well, and when she was old enough, she and David often had great times playing games. She was very patient with him. In his frustration to complete the game and his frustration with her not getting "it," he would often grab the controller out of her hand, with a "Lissa… like this!" She would, for the most part, just let him take it, although she would often also get frustrated, slap him, and then walk off to start something else. He didn't seem to notice when she walked away, and it didn't appear to bother him. In his mind, she only hindered his ability to complete the next level.

As the years progressed, we continually updated the computer. With each subsequent purchase, David would be engrossed in how a new game or program worked, mastering even the most intricate, complex problem within a matter of hours. He could remember long and complicated moves in the game and this helped him to "master" each level, one after the other. His memory in this area was amazing, because computer games didn't require "learning" only a great deal of "remembering" in order to win the game.

At his day care center, small computers were introduced into the classroom, with a number of educational games. David loved this time more than any other and became very good at remembering how to answer the questions each of the programs would ask. However, "remembering" how to answer is different from "knowing" the answer.

Similar to his obsession with reading the same books over and over again and his seemingly vast knowledge of certain words, he appeared to only have to play a computer game for a little while before he was able to master the game quickly. This led us to believe that he was actually using cognitive processes to figure out words and strategies. As his skills developed, he was able to complete every level on every game we had.

It wasn't until many years later that we realized he only had to be shown something once and he could remember it. David remembered words very quickly, so we only had to read a story once and he would remember every word. The books we read at the time were simple, with one or two words per page or a sentence per page, and he could repeat the words verbatim back to us, whilst the book was open on the particular page. However, if we showed him the same word in another book or in another context, he had no idea what the word meant. He could remember the word, but not necessarily the meaning.

But we wouldn't realize that for many years to come.

SCHOOL

Toward the end of 1989, we began researching preschool and school options.

We were already aware David was very different, and although the label "Gifted and Talented" was discussed a lot, nothing, other than his obsession with computers and his knowing his colors and numbers, suggested that "Gifted and Talented and Misunderstood" was in fact the issue.

We attended a number of Gifted and Talented Association meetings; however, he was not in the slightest bit interested in dinosaurs, space travel, insects, or Pythagoras, nor the many varied topics that were themes of the association's events.

A friend of mine suggested we look into Steiner Education. It seemed like the perfect solution.

In the world of Steiner Education, children were guided to make choices about their education, and for us, as parents, it was a whole new and very comfortable approach to the business of learning. As it would happen, a new Steiner school was being built in a beautiful rural setting about forty minutes from where we lived. The parents involved in the creation of this new school were very dedicated and focused on creating a nurturing, peaceful environment for the children and we jumped at the opportunity to enroll David. We were concerned he wouldn't fit into a normal school routine so the idea of self-directed learning and a child-guided approach to education made sense to us.

Gerry and I believed very strongly in children directing their own learning. Neither of us had enjoyed school very much and consequently did not have much faith in the education system, so an alternative education system seemed ideal. Steiner also believed children should not be formally taught how to read until the age of seven—or when their baby teeth started to fall out.

Secretly, I was somewhat relieved. At five, David was developmentally behind the other children in the preschool room at the day care center, and I thought, or reasoned, that perhaps this was the answer.

However, Steiner Education was, in one word, a disaster for us.

While other children thrived on the freedom, David was lost. With no routines, abstract theories and self-directional learning had absolutely the opposite effect on our child. As much as I loved the concept of Steiner and watched in amazement and with a little envy at the way the other children responded to this educational style, for us, it only created more stress.

David struggled to fit in and every time I picked him up from school, there was another story, another complaint from another parent. It became unbearable to even pull into the school's driveway.

What was this?

At home, he was fine, as long as we did the same things every day. He ate well, as long as it was the same thing every day—the same cereal, the same type of apples, chicken, and 'colored noodles' with grated cheese and sliced carrots. He enjoyed any type of dessert – as long as it had lemon in it! Our mornings and nights were, as I realize now, very routine. We did the same thing every day.

Up at 6:30 a.m. and as long as he got dressed, he could play with his Brio train set, an expensive but well-crafted wooden train set he was obsessed with especially since one of the engines looked like Thomas the Tank Engine. We left at the same time every morning and had to take the same route, because he wanted to see a particular set of traffic lights on a certain corner.

Once, deciding there was too much traffic, I tried a different route—forty minutes in the car listening to the mantra of "Traffic lights; no traffic lights today?" from the backseat nearly drove me crazy. The next morning, we took the old route yet again.

Even our music was the same every morning. He loved the popular Australian children's entertainers at the time: Don Spencer and Peter Coombes. I recall many times when I would be driving down the highway, having dropped David off at Steiner and Alissa off at day care, and not registering the tape was still playing, would be singing *"Newspaper, mamma, newspaper mamma, every day!"* a favorite Peter Coombes song at the time, all by myself!

Life was routine and organized, but at the same time, it was spiraling out of control.

Although we persisted as long as we could, we finally had to admit the "experiment" wasn't working, and after six months at Steiner, it was time to admit defeat.

I was heartbroken. I loved the philosophy of the Steiner schools; the gentle way in which learning was introduced into a child's life and the way the parents were involved in the process. It was a beautiful education system; it just didn't work for our child.

One of the many lessons I learned along the way was in trusting my intuition and realizing not everything I thought was a good idea actually was.

School now became a drama. Where on earth were we going to send him to school?

Once again, an alternative was presented to us, which at the time, seemed like a last-minute, rushed decision, but in hindsight, I realized it was, in fact, just the perfect solution.

My cousin suggested a small Catholic school not far from our house. Again, this raised many issues for us; both Gerry and I were raised Catholics, but neither one of us practiced the faith. Both of us had had intensely negative experiences in the Catholic system, me having been educated at a ladies convent all my life, raised by nuns who believed corporal punishment and denial of sexuality were the only true ways to raise girls. Gerry's experience was a little more profound—his memories of walking to Mass at six o'clock on a winter's morning in the prairies of Saskatchewan, Canada, in minus-30-degree temperatures to "attend Church or go to hell" certainly damaged his view of Catholicism.

However, we were desperate. I phoned the school and made an appointment with the principal, a lovely, kind, and caring man who admitted David as the last enrollment they could take for the following year.

It was another blessing in disguise that would not surface for another few years to come.

THE ASSESSMENT AND THE REALITY CHECK

I was really terrified about David going to school. There were so many things different about him. I still remember the special needs teacher, Patty, saying to me, "Really, he is on the borderline. I am not sure if he is ready for school yet."

What on earth are you talking about? I thought, didn't say! This child is a genius; he knows his numbers, his colors; he reads books and can tell me word for word what is written. He has mastered computer games since he was three. What on earth do you mean borderline? Of course, he does have issues with coordination, socialization, and following directions. Again, I believed that this was developmental and that in perhaps a more structured environment, David would thrive…wouldn't he? This was again another instance of me being totally removed from the reality of who David was.

As an educator, Patty saw his difficulty in processing new information. She saw he lacked the fine motor skills to hold a pencil or to color in and his inability to socialize with the other children would hold him back from learning the necessary skills in social development that come with children's early education.

Gerry and I, as first time parents, who believed in the Gifted and Talented tag, saw this as yet another part of the limits of education: not being capable of dealing with gifted students. Gifted children have to figure it out for themselves. We still saw David as educationally gifted, but frustrated. There is no doubt he is certainly intelligent, but we were running on a different wavelength from the educators. Not knowing what was ahead within the education system, we couldn't see that the difficulties David was experiencing were, in fact, hindrances to his ability to learn and that they were, in fact, not normal.

These days parents are more aware of differences. Autism and Asperger's syndrome especially are now identified much earlier. But this was 1991; acceptance and understanding of autistic spectrum disorders, and the tests to screen for developmental differences were still a number of years away. We were on our own, and it was going to be a bumpy ride.

BULLYING—THE BEGINNING

On the day David started school, I was so nervous—and so was he.

At breakfast, beautifully dressed and looking incredibly smart and handsome in his school uniform, he sat at the breakfast table with cereal in his bowl, just looking at it. "What's wrong, David?" I asked. "My tummy feels really funny," he said with a quizzical look on his face. "Don't worry, darling; mine does too," I replied.

And with a big hug, lots of photos, and a backpack filled with the important things in life—a sandwich, a green apple, a drink bottle, and some colored pencils—my beautiful son commenced on, what I believed, was going to be the joyful and exciting school journey. Oh, how wrong I was!

The first day of school for the first child, in any parent's life, is a very exciting, but very scary time. Gerry and I had so many expectations for our firstborn son. School was the first step in a continuum: first school, then graduation, then success. This was how it was supposed to be.

But I was more nervous than most parents on that first day. I realized that there were so many things that he needed reassurance about, that did not come naturally to him; like where to go to find the toilets; what time lunch was what he could buy at the canteen, and how to ask for what he wanted. He needed to know the bell sounded at a certain time and what he was expected to do. I knew already that figuring out these things were not part of David's natural world. It was very important for him to have prior knowledge. I was so worried those at this institution would never know this about him. But other, more experienced parents reassured me that this was normal and that he would only take an hour or two to understand the school routine.

I tried as much as I could to feel comfortable in the knowledge that I was perhaps just an over reactive parent. Perhaps I was not giving him the benefit of the doubt. Perhaps I was just one of those parents who believed nobody really understood my child, and I left my son that morning in the hands of educators who reassured me that, in fact, he would be fine. I felt comforted and terrified all at the same time.

But it didn't take long for me, and those more experienced than me, to realize there was in fact something very different about this child. As much as he tried, David just could not fit in. Coloring was boring. Writing was slow, cumbersome, and too hard. Sitting still with twenty-eight other little people in a hot classroom with a teacher reading a book that had absolutely no relevance to him was just a painful experience.

David would often get up from the mat, where the children were asked to sit and listen to stories, and wander outside. The noise the fans made, the sound of other kids laughing, a bird singing outside the classroom—or any other seemingly minor distraction—made concentrating on what the teacher was saying too difficult for David.

School classrooms are noisy places at the best of times, but any outside noise and distraction occurring when he was supposed to be focusing on work were the biggest issues for David. He was unable to block out outside distractions like other children could. So not only did he find it difficult to concentrate if there was too much noise going on, if he thought the noise

52

outside might be something more interesting or if it was something out of the ordinary, then he needed to go investigate. So if it meant getting up from his desk, or his place on the mat, in the middle of a story or some direction, then so be it. No reasonable explanation any adult came up with could make him understand otherwise.

The educational expectations of the day-to-day school environment made no sense to David; being asked to write stories about how he felt or about what he did on the weekends was just a huge waste of his time in his mind. Coloring in pictures or being expected to color "inside the lines of the drawing" was inconsequential; it made no sense to him, so he just would not conform to those requests.

However, there were certain times of the day he just loved. Playtime and lunchtime were the best, not to play with others but to bury himself in the sand pit, pushing his arms and legs into the soft sand, or to make up imaginary games in his mind, usually involving Thomas the Tank Engine.

He would often take his toy cars and trucks to school so he could make roads in the sand. But it didn't take long for other kids to realize that they would get an explosive reaction if they took his toys. They thought it was funny to take his cars and hide them and watch him retaliate. In an effort to stop it happening, it was suggested he not bring his own toys to school to play with. So then he started playing with sticks and stones, using them as pseudo-trains and trucks.

Some days he found rocks that looked just like Thomas— those were good days. But some days, other children, wanting to play with him, would try to join him in his special games. They would try to introduce rocks or twigs that didn't look like Thomas or The Fat Controller (a character from the show *Thomas the Tank Engine*)—those were the bad days.

On those days, David, unfortunately, reacted often the only way he could: physically. He didn't have the verbal skills to tell people to leave him alone. While he was playing, he was usually so absorbed in his game that it annoyed him immensely if somebody interrupted his train of thought. So he would do what he wanted to say. Instead of asking others to leave him alone, he pushed them out of the way, because, in his mind this meant the same thing!

So, regularly, I was called to the school to talk about a behavioral plan or to reassess and review what he was doing because he had "chosen to respond inappropriately."

Because he wouldn't color in he was sent to the special education classroom, where the wonderfully, patient teacher would sit with him for hours, patiently and kindly trying to get to know him. But coloring in was still stupid in his mind! Likewise, when he reacted to intrusions when he was playing, he was often sent to the vice principal to "think" about what he had done. Nobody seemed to understand however that, in David's mind, he had absolutely no idea how to respond differently, so thinking about it made no difference.

If somebody annoyed him, he reacted the best way he knew how. There was always a story going on in his mind, and often he would be acting out, in his mind, entire scripts of shows he had watched. So, if somebody interrupted his train of thought, then he responded in the best way he could – and unfortunately that often meant physically. Reasoning with him didn't seem to make any difference.

However, because David did act differently than others and because he spent so much time on his own, he then became the kid the others picked on, made fun of, or set up just so they could watch his reactions.

It was a perfect situation for a bully.

David was often slow to understand what was going on, or he would misunderstand the actions of others. This, compounded with his inability to express himself verbally, meant he was the one who was often in trouble, with the bully (or bullies in David's case) feigning innocence or making up a story that appeared to be the truth.

So, while initially I believed we were raising Attila the Hun, one particular incident allowed me to see the pattern and make some sense of what he was going through.

One afternoon, I pulled up to the roundabout outside of the school to pick David up. As I drove up the driveway, I saw a young boy, who was David's friend, standing next to him, with blood on his shirt. David's teacher took him by the hand and walked toward me in the car. I sat and watched, with a sickening, dead feeling of dread in the pit of my stomach. Before his teacher even said a word, I knew what had happened. "David punched another child today, and it is just not acceptable. David is on a behavioral plan, and instead of lining up each morning outside the classroom, he is to meet me in the staff room every day next week," she said.

I was horrified and suitably apologetic. While driving home, I kept going over and over in my mind how I was going to handle this. I didn't want to discipline David in the car, but waited until we got home to talk to him.

But before I could even deal with the situation in a calm and logical sense, as I walked in the door at home, with tears welling up in my eyes and believing I must be the worst parent in the world, the phone was ringing.

I answered it.

"Hello, Mrs. Thibault, its Jimmy's mother here. Your David punched my son today, and I would like to know what measure of discipline you are going to hand out to David?"

I was so apologetic to her and promised David would apologize to her son the next day. I hung up the phone and my heart hurt. Something wasn't right.

I sat with David that night and talked about dealing with confrontational issues. I kept asking David what had happened and he kept replying with the same answer—"He annoys me and makes me angry"—but I couldn't get to the bottom of the issue. With his limited vocabulary, David couldn't find the words to help me understand what was happening. I just gave up and believed that perhaps it was David overreacting to something not really serious at all. How wrong I was.

The issues with Jimmy went on for days, and every afternoon Jimmy's mother called.

"Look," I said finally after apologizing every afternoon, "I will do my best. Are you sure Jimmy isn't doing something to provoke David?"

"Absolutely not," she replied. "My Jimmy is a shy, quiet, and very reserved child, and we expect nothing but exceptional manners in our house. I am not sure where David has learned to solve his issues by using violence, but in our house, we don't resort to that type of discipline!"

I moved from fear and insecurity to fight-or-flight mode. The anger bubbled up inside of me. "Look, Jane," I said, "I don't know what you are implying here, but I can assure you we do not use violence in our house. Can you just ask Jimmy to stay away from David altogether?"

"Oh," she replied in a very superior manner, "Don't you worry about that. I am going to see the vice principal tomorrow to demand that David be expelled!"

With that, she hung up. I was angry, scared, and heartbroken. My child was only a few weeks into Year 1 of school and already a parent was demanding he be expelled!

What on earth were we doing wrong? At home, David was a little unruly, but for the most part, he was kind and considerate, joyful, and intelligent. Was I really the worst mother in the world? Had I totally screwed up this whole parenting thing?

I couldn't eat dinner that night, I felt ill. I tossed and turned all night replaying the conversation over and over in my mind.

By 4 a.m., I had the solution. I was going to get to school early and see the vice principal before Jane got there, and then I was going to watch what happened next.

At 7:25, I was sitting outside the vice principal's office. Nobody was going to have my child expelled.

At 7:32, I was sitting in the office crying. All the words, all the sentences, all the "I am not going to put up with this woman calling me" dissolved as soon as I opened my mouth.

The vice principal was one of those very experienced, very caring teachers who had obviously dealt with hysterical, over-reactive first-year parents for many years. He sat there, patiently and understandingly listening to this hysterical woman (me) describe, in detail, the events of the previous week and listened with a kind look on his face to my concerns my Year 1 son was heading for expulsion.

Finally, after the story was out and I had run out of words, he took a deep breath and said, "Yes. We believe David is not entirely at fault and, in fact, have actually told Jane we believe Jimmy is antagonizing the situation. She is an emotional person, and no, David is not going to be expelled."

I could have hugged him. He was so patient and understanding and had such tact in dealing with an overtired, very stressed, and inexperienced, year-one parent who hadn't had a lot of sleep the night before. I felt much better as I left his office and headed for David's classroom.

I positioned myself a fair way from where the children were standing outside their classroom, because I wanted to see for myself just what on earth went on every morning.

Each morning, the children were expected to line up outside their classroom to wait for their teacher to arrive. David had positioned himself at the head of the line. The other children were laughing and talking with each other. David, on the other hand, was in his own world. As more children started to line up behind him and were still talking and interacting, he was not taking any notice of them. He was totally involved in some story going on in his head. Jimmy's mother dropped him at the classroom, and then she headed off in the direction of the vice principal's office. Huh, I thought, beat you to it, lady!

Childish, I know, but I was grasping at straws.

Jimmy sat down on the brick wall outside the classroom, opposite the classroom door, and waited and watched. While all the other kids were lined up behind David, chatting and talking, David stood at the front of the line, still in his own world, totally oblivious to anything else around him.

I could see his teacher coming down the path. Jimmy could as well. And perfectly timed for maximum impact, as she turned around the corner, Jimmy stood up, walked right in front of David, stepped on his toes, and pushed him so David fell back onto the other kids.

David reacted by pushing him back with a "Jimmy, I was here first." Then, just as his teacher walked up to the line, Jimmy, with one eye on her, turned to David and said, "David! Stop pushing me, I was here first." With that David shoved him again.

The teacher looked straight at David who was glaring at Jimmy and said. "David, how many times have I told you to stop pushing Jimmy; that was really unkind? Stand at the back."

David just stood there, dumbfounded. He didn't have the words to retaliate, his eyes filled with tears, and some of the kids laughed and pointed at him. Not Jimmy, however; he walked into the classroom with a smug, superior grin—holding the teachers hand.

Got it, you little bastard, I thought. Again, childish I know, but victory was just around the corner, and I couldn't wait for 3:30 that afternoon.

Sure enough, the phone was ringing when I walked in the door. "Hello," I said, knowing full well who it was.

"Hello, Sally. It's Jane. Your David has been at my Jimmy again. I have been to see the vice principal, and I will go and see him tomorrow. And if I can't get satisfaction, I am going to the Parents & Friends Association to get them to have him removed. We just can't have children like David at this school; it gives the whole school a bad name."

Battle stations, all guns pointed, loaded and ready to go. "Now just a minute Jane, just when did David 'have a go' at

Jimmy today?" I said slowly with a feeling of smug satisfaction, but with my heart beating so loud and fast that I thought it was going to burst right out of my chest.

"In the line where he always does," was her supercilious response.

I took a deep breath and stood as tall as I possibly could, even though she was on the phone, I needed to feel strong. My hands were shaking, but I wasn't going to let that stop me. "Actually Jane, I stood and watched the children line up today, and I can tell you it was actually Jimmy who started it. David was standing in the line, and he pushed in, stood on David's toes, and then shoved him.

"I have already spoken to David's teacher and to the vice principal, and they know the story. So I would suggest to you, Jane, that rather than making judgments about other parents' behaviors, you would look at your son and perhaps question him as to why he feels, first, he has to bully an innocent child and, second, why he feels such joy in making somebody else miserable. Tell Jimmy to stay away from David. I will be watching every morning."

I hung up and never spoke to the woman again.

I poured myself a big glass of wine and sat down—my heart thumping, my hands shaking. Why did this feel like it wouldn't be the last time I would have to step over the line to defend my child?

SCHOOL DAYS

School for David became a pattern: some days good; most days, not so good. But in retrospect, I have realized the "good days/years" really depended on which teacher he had and his or her ability to intuitively understand and accept David for who he was.

In Year 2, his teacher was wonderful. David loved her, and because he loved her so much, there were very few incidents in the classroom. Anne just seemed to know how to kindly and efficiently handle any incident that occurred, without making judgment.

Realizing he couldn't read aloud as well as the other children, she never put him in a situation where he had to do it. So, when it was David's turn to read to her, she would let him sit on her lap to hear the story. She didn't seem to mind and he loved it. Anne had a wonderful way of just connecting with David. She seemed to intuitively know when he needed to go out for a break from class, and so she assigned him the "message bearer." If a note needed to go to the office or a message to another teacher, she was always very careful to explain exactly where he was to go, who he was to see, and what he was supposed to do.

There was only one incident where he got lost. So she assigned two kind girls as David's carers, who became like his guardian angels. Their job was to take turns accompanying him on message errands, to remind him when he had to get changed out of his school uniform and into his sports uniform for sports afternoons, and to remind him where he was supposed to be going, and they often helped him to write his stories. They loved looking after him, and he thought they were just wonderful. I will be eternally grateful to the three of them for helping make David's second year at school a far happier experience than his first.

Year 2 was also very special as David became friends with three boys, and the foursome quickly became friends, although mostly out of school. They were all laid back, easygoing kids who seemed to accept David's eccentricities without question. Besides, with his extraordinary memory for all things involving computer games, he was able to memorize all the "cheats" and could help them win at computer games, David was a great friend to have!

But as each year wore on, the bullying and his ability to keep up with his classmates became more and more distinct. His core group of buddies were great, and because I was good friends with their mothers, they were mostly after-school friends.

David still found interacting in the playground difficult because of the noise and the unpredictable movements by the other children, and preferred to play alone during morning and lunch breaks. However, being on his own made him a target for bullying, which became nastier as he got older. Verbally, David still found it very difficult to communicate, and so he withdrew even further into his own world.

As he became older, David's concentration and inability to process information began to cause him to fall seriously behind in his schoolwork. The situation began to compound, and warning bells were ringing every day.

THE BULLYING INTENSIFIES

David's difficulties with his school work were ongoing and at times very confusing. His learning support teacher, Patty, was gentle and kind and had what I could only describe as a sixth sense when it came to dealing with David.

I spent many long hours with Patty trying to understand what was going on. She and I both were dealing with such an unknown. How could this gentle, intelligent, funny child have so many learning issues to deal with? Although nothing David did fitted a particular model, in partnership, we tried many different options. Every now and then, David would make a breakthrough that would give him some sense of achievement and success. We would use that success to build on the next step.

It reminded me a little of a story I heard many years later about how many times a space shuttle is actually on and off course when on a mission. Often, depending on all sorts of situations, the navigator has to make major and minor adjustments to keep the shuttle on course. It was the same for us. We would just make an academic breakthrough, thinking that this time we had figured out what was going on, then something would happen, causing a setback, and we would have to go back to square one again.

What I didn't realize at the time was that a far bigger issue was evolving. David was being bullied often, and because of his limited vocabulary, he kept most incidents to himself because he would not and, in some cases could not, explain what was happening. He would often internalize incidents rather than deal with them or seek help.

The bullies, I came to realize, were both smart and sneaky. Many times, they would choose places or situations where it was difficult for adults to witness or to really understand exactly what was going on.

On the flip side of this, many adults didn't know what to do to solve bullying and so would either pretend that nothing had happened or minimize the seriousness of the incident. This would cause great consternation for David because, as I realize now, the incidents were never handled with continuity. There was no standard framework or disciplinary measures that he could understand because each incident, although the same in his mind, appeared to be different to others.

Sometimes, the bullies were dealt with, and sometimes (most times), they were not. Sometimes, David got an apology, and sometimes (most times), he did not. Sometimes (most times), David got into trouble for reacting because the adult didn't see what had happened.

If David was caught fighting with somebody or responding inappropriately toward another child, the teachers would bring both parties into the school office to explain the situation. The teachers would then listen to the stories from the bullies and the partial version from David, and often took the bully's version as being accurate, because it was easier to understand. David's language skills were limited and he could usually only respond with the words "they were annoying me."

The outcome was usually a discipline measure handed out to David, him having to apologize to the bullies and then having to deal with the snickering and giggling from the perpetrators as they walked out of the office. The result was

David learned not to say anything—it was too confusing to be honest.

If I became aware of a situation and asked him to tell me what happened, he would often just tell me that he wanted to deal with things by himself and that he wouldn't "dob!" *Dob* is an Australian term used when friends won't tell on each other. In some ways, David felt that by not dobbing, he was being strong. Somewhere he had read or somebody had told him about the term *dobbing*, and he had taken it in its most literal sense, even if it meant he would be hurt physically or emotionally in the process.

Although there were many incidents during this time, one in particular stands out.

After school on this particular afternoon, I was waiting for David at our usual spot for afternoon pickup. After about ten minutes, I parked the car and went to look for him. Punctuality is very important to David, and being ten minutes late was akin to being an hour late for most people. Something was wrong.

I eventually found David in a very distressed state. Four boys had thought it would be funny to take David's schoolbag and hide it. I found him in his classroom attempting to tell his teacher about his lost schoolbag. He was beside himself, and the teacher, without success, was trying to get him to explain what had happened.

As I arrived, one of the students from the classroom below brought David's bag up from the ground floor of the building. The boys from his class had taken his bag out of the bag racks outside of his classroom and had hidden it in the bag racks outside the classroom directly below his. One of the girls had seen the boys standing behind a tree laughing and had figured out what was going on.

The teacher confronted the boys and brought them up to the classroom to get the boys to apologize to David. They did so, reluctantly and with smirks on their faces. David kept asking why they were so mean to him, and even though the teacher questioned why the boys hid David's bag, they just shrugged and said they thought it was funny to watch him get upset.

Those boys tormented David for the rest of the year: throwing rocks and stones at him when nobody was looking, running past him and bumping into him so he would react. They took great joy in watching him lose it emotionally. They made fun of him all the time, and with his limited vocabulary and understanding of social cues, he would often respond in inappropriate ways.

For me, it was a very difficult time. I could tell when things were not right. He would get in the car some afternoons and I just knew something had happened. But when I would ask if everything was OK, he would shrug or say, "It's OK; nothing happened." Pushing for more information often made him more emotional. So on many days, I would just have to let him deal with it and hope the day had been OK and the bullying had been bearable. Those days broke my heart.

THE TURNING POINT

One day, in a story retold to me by one of the teachers, David did stand up to the bullies. And it was a great turning point for him.

At the morning break, David was standing out in a quiet area he liked to go to. One of his de-stressing rituals was to grab a big stick and walk around a tree, trailing the stick behind him, a routine that became very much a part of David's life both at school and at home. David was usually off in his own world at the time, creating stories in his head or just, what I came to term, debriefing.

The "Gang of Four" began stalking him again, throwing stones just so they would land at his feet. They would then run and hide so he would look up, be distracted, become agitated, and start to look around for the culprit before returning to his story.

The teacher positioned himself just far enough away so that neither David nor the boys knew he was observing them. He watched for a while and, as he told me later, so wanted David to punch one of them, "just not too hard." Although he wanted David to react, he also didn't want David to place himself in a situation where he would be in trouble for his actions. It was a fine line, and he was ready to step in at the right time. He felt that if David could just stand up for himself, just this once, perhaps the boys would leave him alone.

Sure enough, after a few minutes of taunting, David lost it, picked up the stick, and went after them. He cornered one boy and, with the stick raised behind him, yelled, "Just leave me alone!"

The teacher told me later that he started to run toward David, saying to himself, "Don't hit him, David; please don't hit him," but at the same time, he was so thrilled that David had finally stood up for himself.

The outcome was perfect. The boys were shocked and speechless. David had stood up to them and they backed down. All of a sudden, David's response wasn't so funny. They were scared and he had finally called their bluff.

We had rehearsed the scenario at home many times, practicing over and over how to use his words, rather than his actions, to tell people what he wanted. I was so excited it had actually paid off, and sure enough, the boys had backed down, and so began a few months with no bullying incidents.

BEAN-BAG TIME

During this time, Gerry and I developed a number of rituals to ensure we spent time helping David to de-stress each evening. One of those rituals was our nightly "bean bag" time.

Every night, David would spend a great deal of time in his room either reading his Thomas the Tank Engine books and, later, the Power Rangers books or playing with his Brio train set. The Brio train set was a series of wooden train tracks and accessories that linked together to form a massive train line. They were very expensive, but we figured that if he was going to play with this set as often as he did, then we wanted him to play with wood, rather than plastic. For years, the Brio train tracks snaked through his bedroom, forming all sorts of shapes. David would then spend hours re-creating Thomas the Tank Engine stories in his room.

Later on, we moved a computer into his room so he could play games. Gerry would often play a game with him, and I liked to talk or just be with him, so I bought two bean bags for his room.

Our bean-bag time became a bit of a ritual as at night; after Alissa had gone to bed, either Gerry or I would sit in one bean bag and David in the other, reading, building another train configuration, or playing games on the computer.

Some nights he would talk about his day and often tell me about things the other kids had said or done. Not in great detail, but I eventually figured out how to piece together snippets of information—enough to realize school life for him was very challenging.

But one particular night, just after the incident with the Gang of Four, he got up from his bean bag and moved it close to mine so he could move most of his body into my bean bag. I put my arm around him so we could sit still and cuddle.

This was not a common occurrence, and I was a bit surprised that he wanted to just sit quietly. I stayed perfectly still and just held him for what seemed like a wonderful eternity. I was so enjoying just being close to him in the silence, just he and I together.

After about ten minutes or so, he asked very quietly, "Mum, why do friends make you feel so sad?"

My heart broke. "Darling, friends are not supposed to make you feel sad. They make you feel happy, you know, like when you went to Lucas's house that day and swam in the pool, or the time that you stayed at Adam's house and played computer games."

"Oh," he said. "But mostly they make you feel sad, don't they?"

The dagger that lived permanently in my heart, twisted again.

LIFE BECOMES MORE INTENSE

Toward David's second year of school, we were really struggling financially. We had invested in a number of property deals when the bank interest rates went to 22 percent.

I was working part-time at the gym and was looking to go back to university to do a teaching degree, and Gerry was struggling to hold onto the properties and still sell real estate in "the recession we had to have," so eloquently quoted by our Treasurer of Australia at the time!

Times had been great, but now it was getting tough, and being first time in the real estate game, neither one of us knew anything about real estate "cycles." Gerry was an excellent salesman and has a very quick logic. Having a great ability to see a deal when there wasn't one, he became one of the top commercial real estate salespeople on the Gold Coast.

However, while the good years were fabulous, when the tide turned, it was like a tsunami! As interest rates went higher, the phones stopped ringing and the sales dried up. Little by little, we had to sell; bit by bit, we had to cut back, cut down, and change habits. That, on top of trying to come to terms with David's difference, was placing a huge strain on our marriage.

There were many nights of arguing, slamming doors, and walking out. I was really struggling with understanding who I was, what I was doing, and what I brought to our relationship and to motherhood. Who was I? One minute, I had had a dream; the next minute, it was a nightmare.

In my dream, life was calm, peaceful, and joyful. There was a picket fence along the front of a pretty house with lace curtains. In my dream, our lives were bliss. We traveled, we socialized, and we entertained. We were both successful entrepreneurs with fabulously successful businesses and fabulously successful children.

In reality, the nightmare that was our life was overpowering the dream. The picket fence had fallen. There were no lace curtains; in fact, it felt like our lives were 'on show' in front of very big windows! We travelled a little, but if you call a picnic every Sunday out in the park travelling, then we did lots! We entertained somewhat, but most times I was beside myself with worry or concern for David and for Gerry, so although we had great friends, it was difficult for me to be myself; I was always second-guessing everything I did.

My grip on life was loosening. What I believed about mothering and parenting was in total discord with reality. I loved my children to bits, but this was so hard. There didn't seem to be anytime when I wasn't worried or concerned or on edge. My life and my beliefs were in constant flux. I truly believed in the power of positive thinking, but real life and real incidents were not matching what I thought I believed, and I felt that I was never in a place of calm.

Gerry was desperately trying to hang onto what little we had left and although he was a brilliant sales person, the property market at the time took a huge nosedive and along with it a number of properties we had invested in.

We were on a collision course. We were so caught up trying to survive that we were missing some of the many opportunities that arise in times of turmoil. We began to believe that we were failures, not only in business but also as parents. Nothing we seemed to do would work. Everything was hard. It was like living in black sludge. We just went from bad to worse, and our world was closing in on us.

I had enrolled to do a Bachelor of Education program, believing that if I understood teaching a little better, perhaps I could help David. However, something else changed, and at the beginning of 1993, at the start of David's third year of school, I discovered that I was pregnant.

Gerry was concerned about our finances—justifiably so—we had none, but at the same time, for some reason, I believed that this new baby heralded a change in our family. I just knew that somehow, this baby, who was determined to be conceived despite all precautions, obviously had a role to play in our family. So I embraced this pregnancy with all the joy and hope that had come with our previous two children.

"We will survive" became my mantra, and besides, I had always wanted more than two children. I would often look at family photos of Gerry, David, Alissa, and I and think that our family was not complete yet. So here was our little 'full stop' that came after the words "our family."

When I reached the three-month mark, Gerry and I told David and Alissa. "Well done, Mum" said David! Alissa was desperate for a little sister; she had grown into a beautiful little social butterfly with many friends, and the thought of a little sister to play with twenty-four hours a day was just wonderful.

And so, on November 1, 1993, our little Scorpio, Caitlin, entered the world—and never before has a little sister been loved so much by a brother and sister. They were absolutely taken with Caitlin.

David adored her and would often come into our room at night and just watch her sleep. He couldn't wait for her to wake up in the morning and say something or do something so he could get to school to tell everybody about his baby sister. Alissa became a little mother and naturally became my little helper, always at my side whenever Caitlin needed to be picked up or needed a diaper change. They just loved her.

However, amid all of this, financially, we were done. The recession was starting to bite hard, and the real estate industry was in a huge downward spiral. Large commissions were no longer coming in. We were finally forced to sell our house, just before the bank foreclosed, to pay off as many debts as we could and move into a rented house. This was a time of great struggle and stress for us, where much of what we owned we sold, which left us with very little that we could call our own.

If somebody had asked me to recount those days, I would have said in fact they were very sad times and unhappy times. But it is funny how our memories work. When researching this book, I pulled out all the videos taken during that time, and I must admit to being very surprised at how, in those very stressful times, we managed, as a family, to create a life of fun and laughter in among all the financial turmoil.

The videos were usually of just us interacting on a day to day basis. Sometimes the children were swimming in the pool; sometimes they were of us all dancing in the living room. But they relayed something very important; the family connection we developed in the most simplest of activities.

David and Alissa had the most amazing relationship and an extremely protective relationship toward Caitlin. David and Alissa were like little twin souls. David relied on Alissa to non-verbally help him with what was the right thing to do. Alissa's warmth and laughter made him feel safe, and he adored her. They played together all the time, making up imaginary games with cubby houses made out of sheets, spending hours in the swimming pool being all sorts of imaginary animals, living in all sorts of worlds. Life together for just the two of them, with baby Caitlin in tow, was full of great adventures, all played out in our backyard.

Caitlin and Alissa taught David how to be gentle and kind and how to treat women with care and consideration. Girls are to be treated differently than are boys, and both of his sisters inherently knew their roles were to help David become a gentle, thoughtful man who, to this day, treats women with respect and kindness, a quality in him we are exceptionally proud of.

SPORT

Finding activities for David to participate in was always a challenge. He really enjoyed playing soccer, but as it was a team sport, he found it very challenging.

Although he was loved to wear his uniform and soccer boots and couldn't wait to get to practice, his ability to stay focused during a game was limited.

Because of his motor skills challenges, he often played in the goalie position. But standing in the goals for minutes on end, watching the play at the other end of the field, made it very difficult for him to stay present and focused. Many times, when the ball would be coming towards him, he would be standing in the goal, playing with the net, and not paying the slightest bit of attention to the game, much to the frustration of his coach and the other players.

David didn't really care about the game or increasing his skills. There were far too many things to create in his head. But he liked being involved and having the interaction with the other boys, even if they only occasionally kicked the ball to him!

However, even though there were often frustrating moments, there were also many funny moments during our soccer days.

Playing in the under-sevens team meant that the boys played first on Saturday mornings, with the games often starting at 8 a.m. On one very cold Saturday morning, as finally the ball was coming down the field, David was engrossed on something on the ground. We, as usual, were standing along the sidelines, like all the other parents. As the ball started to head in the direction of where David was standing, we all started to yell, "David, watch the ball," when one of the members of the other team had a breakaway. He lined up for a kick that looked like it was going to land right in the center of the goal—perfectly placed for David to stop it.

"David, the ball is coming," we started yelling. "David!"

He looked up, just as the ball sailed past him, and the opposition yelled in triumph at scoring a goal.

David was looking straight at us, oblivious to his team members yelling at him. He held up his hand and said, "Look, Mum; this rock looks just like an airplane."

OK, so goalie was not the right position. Let's try wing.

So, the next Saturday, once again, we were standing along the sidelines cheering on the team. This time, David was playing on the wing. At one point, he was running for the ball, and it looked like it just might happen—the ball and his boot might just connect. We were jumping up and down on the sideline, so excited. "Go David, Go!" we were all yelling.

Alissa especially was cheering and yelling the loudest. As he ran past us, he stopped, saw Alissa cheering so excitedly for him, ran to her, and gave her a big hug!

The finals rolled around, and David sat on the bench throughout the match. "The team has a great chance of winning the final," his coach had said. "And many other parents are frustrated when David plays, so he will sit out the game today." David was heartbroken. I was furious.

So the soccer boots were retired to the bottom of the cupboard until many years later, when soccer became an important part of his life and he was able to experience great success.

TAE KWON DO—THE FIRST GREAT WIN

"What about martial arts?" Gerry said one night. "Perhaps that would teach him some discipline and focus?"

Friends of ours had just found a new Tae Kwon Do training center not far from where we lived. So the next week, David and Alissa were off to their first Taekwondo lesson.

They both loved it. David really thrived on the discipline and the no-nonsense way that the instructors spoke. They were incredibly patient, and rules were just rules; they were simple to understand and you just followed them. No question, no challenge. A rule was a rule. It didn't change or waver. Within these parameters, David felt comfortable, and so, although physically he was not as up to speed like the other children, he was able to grasp the concepts and work toward success—he knew exactly what he was aiming for.

David and Alissa, who, I had secretly hoped, would rather wear a tutu than a Tae Kwon Do uniform, spent every Tuesday night learning the skills and discipline involved in mastering a martial art.

After about six months of training, they were both asked to compete in a Taekwondo competition.

Now I was very new to this whole martial arts thing and thought, 'Oh how lovely. They must get up and practice all their moves and be judged on how they execute them.'

So every night, both David and Alissa practiced their round-house kicks and all the other moves constituting the art of Tae Kwon Do.

On the designated Sunday, we arrive at 8 a.m., the children dressed in their uniforms.

"Oh," said their instructor. "Did you remind Mum to get the mouth guards?"

"Mouth guards! Why on earth do they need mouth guards?" I innocently asked.

"So that their teeth don't get knocked out in a kick!" was his indignant answer; the instructor was obviously thinking I was a mother who needed a little help!

"Hang on, what do you mean get knocked out with a kick? Isn't this just a demonstration, showing the moves they have learned?" You could just see him roll his eyes and think, what have we got here?

"No," he said ever so patiently. "They compete with others in numerous fights during the day."

"Fights! Fights! Who said anything about fights?" David and Alissa just looked at me in horror as well.

We are the ultimate greenies and peacemakers; totally focused on peace love and tranquility; what do you mean fights?

I was horrified.

"Mum," Alissa said, "It will be OK. We will be fine." Great, I thought, wise words of wisdom and confidence coming from my eight-year-old!

The next three hours were hell as I watched my beautiful children actually fight: kicking, punching, and performing those roundhouse thingies, which apparently you are judged on. I hated it.

But my two little warriors loved it. I saw in both of them anger and determination I had never seen before.

Alissa's first fight was tough. She got pummeled, but the girl she was fighting happened to hit her in the head (on her helmet, mind you, but a hit to the head it was) and the tiger in Alissa surfaced. She was angry. She won the fight in the last two minutes of the match.

When she came off the mat, she was furious. "Nobody kicks me in the head and gets away with it," she said. "That's when I got really mad." Whoa! Go the redhead—I was seeing that side of her for the first time, and I was pretty sure it wouldn't be the last.

David's first fight, however, was just painful to watch.

He was kicked, punched, and pushed off the mat. One part of me wanted to jump onto the mats and pull him away and kick his opponent and the other part of me was waiting for David, hoping and praying he would somehow get one kick in.

He came off his fight really hurt and was trying so hard not to cry. I wanted to take him home. I wanted to wrap him up in a big hug and just walk out of the stadium. "David, we can go home if you want," I said, as I touched the scrape under his eye.

"No, Mum," he said. "If I go home now, I will never learn to fight back."

My eyes filled with tears. I felt so proud of him. "Well, darling, if that's what you want, but if you need, just call me and I will come and kick your opponent for you, OK?" He wasn't sure if I was serious or not. Believe me I was!

His friend Andrew said, "Come on, David; let's go and do some practice." And with that, he and Andrew went behind the stands, and Andrew patiently gave David some tips and pointers.

Alissa was up next and won her next fight convincingly. She had figured out what she was expected to do, and in no way was she going to let anybody get the better of her again: the tiger had been released!

Then it was David's turn again. Oh please, I thought quietly, just let him get one kick in.

The fight started just like the earlier one. The boy had watched David fight before and knew exactly what to expect.

The first kick landed right in the middle of David's stomach. He was wearing padding, but the sound of the kick was enough to make me cringe in agony. The force of the kick pushed David out of the square, and he landed right on his butt.

He sat there for just a split second, and I saw a total change come over his face.

We were all yelling and cheering for him. He stood up, raised his arms, and glanced at Andrew, who was jumping up and down and cheering him on. He looked back at his opponent, with such a look of determination and his entire posture changed.

He took on a totally different stance: he became confident and powerful. He pummeled his opponent, who was taken off guard and had been, I think, feeling a little smug. David didn't stop until the bell went.

Oh, please, I thought, just let him win this one fight. Just once, let him experience victory. The decision seemed to take forever.

The referee moved into the middle of the mat, grabbed both boys' arms, and, after what seemed like an eternity, raised David's arm up. He had won!

Bedlam ensued in the stands. We were all jumping and cheering and crying at the same time. David couldn't believe it. He ran back to us yelling, "I won! I won!" Never ever before, in the history of any competition anywhere in the world, had a victory been as sweet as this one.

But the afternoon wasn't over. Later they announced the competition winners. Alissa won her division and David was runner-up in his! Both came home with a trophy. We were so excited.

Later that evening, as David and I sat in the bean bags looking at the trophy proudly standing on his dresser, he said, "You know, Mum, I am never ever, ever going to forget this moment."

"David," I replied, "You learned so much today about determination, focus, and getting what you want, but also you learned you can do anything you want. You just have to decide you want it badly enough".

"Yes," he said, suddenly looking about six inches taller. "I am really proud of myself."

"I am so proud of you too, darling," I said, glowing with pride. It could have been a gold medal, I was so proud of him. We sat in the bean bags for a very long time that night.

DISCOVERING THE DIAGNOSIS

In 1996, friends of ours who worked at a university introduced us to the World Wide Web. It was amazing. In its infancy in Australia, the WWW was fast becoming a world of information and contacts never known before.

This could be my answer, I thought. Perhaps something on the Internet could at least point me in the right direction.

So, each day after dropping the kids at school and Caitlin at day care, I would sit at the computer, log onto the Internet, and search for answers.

In 1996, the Internet was a very different place to what it is today. There was no such thing as broadband or a wireless connection. Instead, we had to go via the phone line, and connecting was a long, slow process. Today, we are used to lightning-fast access to a myriad of virtual sites on different topics. Google makes finding information relatively easy; however, in those days, downloading sites and accessing information were often slow, laborious processes, requiring a large amount of intuition and patience to find exactly what you were looking for.

Hence, often I would be on the computer for hours at a time, bouncing from one site to another trying to find information relevant to David and the issues he was dealing with. I would type in all sorts of symptoms, behaviors, and questions to seek information. The searches would often lead to one word: autism!

Each time the word appeared in the search, I would shut the computer down.

At that time, I had only understood those diagnosed with autism as being unable to speak or interact with others and living in an isolated world. It certainly didn't describe David. Although he still found language difficult and didn't understand social nuances, he was funny, intelligent, and interacted with people, albeit with some difficulty. You could, I suppose, describe his sense of humor as quirky, his intelligence singularly focused only on things he was interested in and interactive as long as it was about a computer game or the Power Rangers. By then, the Power Rangers had taken over where Thomas the Tank Engine had left off. Books, games, TV Show, costumes, the Power Rangers took over our house!

My searching skills were not sophisticated then either, so I was often led down one path only to get to the end of the search, realize I was way off track and have to start all over again.

However, one night, in January 1997, I think it must have been around eleven, a website popped up in the search engine called O.A.S.I.S, moderated by the wonderfully patient and knowledgeable Barb Kirby. The website described a new aspect to the autism spectrum called Asperger's syndrome first identified by Hans Asperger in 1944.

Asperger's syndrome, a new term, entered into our vocabulary and, from that night, would become an intrinsic part of our lives.

From that moment on, I knew I had the answer, and I researched everything I could find on the Internet about Asperger's syndrome. This research included numerous e-mails to Barb, who, in hindsight, must have been receiving e-mails from all around the world asking the same questions. But she always answered the e-mails with patience and knowledge. As much as I didn't want to accept it, I knew this was probably the answer we had been seeking.

The more I read, the more the diagnosis fit. I ended up with numerous files of information, much of it downloaded from the many sites popping up on the Internet each week. It was as if Asperger's syndrome and all the information about it had now taken over our lives. After e-mailing many of those involved with the different sites, I began to finally feel we were on the right path. I had found some answers, but I was concerned about where to go next.

Gerry and I spent many nights discussing this new information. Everything started to make sense, but now what?

So, armed with the information, I went to see Patty. A number of things concerned us. We were worried about labeling David; we didn't want to put him in a box, to define him with no way out. I spoke to Patty about our concerns. Would a diagnosis mean he would only live up to those expectations deemed by others? After much discussion, Gerry and I came to realize that if we all knew what we were dealing with, then perhaps the judgments and ignorance dished out by others would dissipate.

Bearing in mind this was 1997 and very little was known about Asperger's syndrome in the Australian education system, this was all new territory. Gerry and I felt like we were on our own. So after weeks of research and soul searching, we no longer had any doubts in our minds what this issue was, and with great trepidation, the journey began.

I contacted the Autistic Society in Brisbane, which recommended a specialist. I then contacted our family doctor and asked him for a referral. Finally we were getting closer to creating some solutions, and I began to feel empowered. Confidence in my parenting abilities and dealing with the medical and education system slowly returned. I was a mother on a mission!

At the same time, I began journaling as a way to sort out and record the many events of the year. It was something I had wanted to do for many years, and quite fortuitously, I had actually gotten my act together during that particular year to do it. In writing this book, I came across my journals and many of the entries took me back to exactly what life was like for us during that time.

The earliest journal entry was just before David's diagnosis.

Saturday, January 11, 1997

I am feeling nervous about David's appointment next Saturday. Both Gerry and I realized he didn't say a word yesterday, just wandered in his own world.

Then he hurt Caitlin because she hurt him. It was as if he had no idea what pain was. He protested he had not hurt her, incredibly adamant about it. Is he just so disconnected from the process? Or is he so connected to something else he doesn't understand his actions will have an effect on somebody?

On Saturday, January 18, with a stack of documentation from every specialist David had seen in twelve years and with pages of downloaded information from the Internet, David and I headed off for, what was to be, a life-changing day.

No, It's not Bad Parenting!

The trip to Brisbane was long. David was very talkative on the way. The appointment was for 10 a.m., so we left at 8:30, just to ensure we would be on-time and to allow for any unforeseen traffic delays. I had waited a long time for this appointment, and I wasn't going to be late.

"Who are we going to see again, Mum?" he asked for the tenth time.

"A really nice man, who might make it a bit easier for you to understand why sometimes things and people are difficult to understand," I said.

"There is nothing wrong with me Mum; it's everybody else," he replied.

The specialist was a kind, soft-spoken man and he welcomed us both into his office. I handed him two folders filled with reports from schools, occupational therapists, speech therapists, and psychologists; behavioral reports; letters from teachers and carers; and reams and reams of information downloaded from the Internet.

He took one look at the file and said, "I think you probably know already what the issue is."

He spoke to David, asked him to answer some questions, and then examined him. He asked me his history, looked at the reports, and spoke to me at length about what life was like for David.

He had questions for me. "Are there any relatives on either you or your husband's side of the family who you would describe as being a little odd or perhaps eccentric?"

My first thought was, where would you like me to start? Both Gerry and I had shared many stories in the past about 'eccentric' relatives in our extended families on both sides. Trying to pick just one would be too difficult!

"Well," he said. "I don't think I am going to tell you anything you don't already know. Yes, David presents as sitting on the autistic spectrum, with what we are coming to know more about, and that is the *diagnosis* of Asperger's syndrome."

I spent the long trip home bouncing from one emotion to the other. I was amazed at how shocked I felt, even though I knew in my heart that Asperger's was the answer.

I was glad we finally had a diagnosis, but at the same time, I was so sad we finally had a diagnosis. I think I had wished in my heart it was, as everybody thought, because we didn't parent properly!

During the drive home, I kept looking at David out of the corner of my eye. I was already planning the neon sign I was going to have erected at the local corner store: "To all you judgmental people who have made me feel like I was doing something wrong all these years: it's called Asperger's syndrome. We are not bad parents!"

The trip was slow. There had been a traffic accident earlier, so the cars were traveling at a snail's pace along the highway. The slowness of the traffic seemed surreal. It was as if life was operating in slow motion so that I had time to process the emotions and thoughts I was feeling.

I was aware of the music on the radio and David chatting about cars and traffic lights, but it was if everything was happening outside of my reality. I felt as if I were not connected to my body, nor that it was the Saturday it was. I was hanging on to the steering wheel for life, thinking it would keep me from just float-ing away. I kept trying to process the words, *"David presents as sitting on the autism spectrum, with what we are coming to know more about, and that is Asperger's syndrome,"* but they felt so surreal.

I was bouncing from one thought to the other. This is for life; this means it is permanent; I can't run from this; I won't wake up tomorrow morning and think, "Well, today he might just grow out of this." This diagnosis meant this was going to be his life, and our lives, for the rest of our lives.

I wanted to cry, but I wanted to laugh from relief. I wanted to scream from the car window, "This is not fair! This is *not* how it should be." On the other hand, I felt a sense of peace because we finally had an answer. I so badly wanted this to be a dream, but now this was our reality. All our searching was over. Now we had to deal with it.

One minute I was being totally rational and adult about the whole thing: 'I can deal with this. This is not the end of the world. I have gotten this far, and I am sure this will all be OK.'

Then next minute, I wanted to scream and cry and run away: 'This is all too hard. I am not grown up enough for this. This happens to other people—people who are far more capable of dealing with this than me. Perhaps there has been a mistake; this isn't the way it is supposed to be!'

While all these thoughts were playing a crazy game of bouncing off the walls of my already overloaded brain, there was something else to contend with – we had something to fix this. The Doctor had prescribed dextroamphetamine, a pill to help make school easier and help David concentrate.

So while I was dealing with the words *Asperger's syndrome*, trying to get my head around the fact those two words were now a part of who we were, I was also imagining what life would be like for us now, with the "wonder" drug.

Could this pill be the answer? Did this mean that, tomorrow morning, David would wake up and not have Asperger's? Would this pill help him stay focused, help him understand people, help stop the bullying?

I had no idea what dextroamphetamine was. I just thought this was going to make David's life easier. So now, on top of every other emotion I was feeling, let's throw excitement into the mix, shall we? I hadn't realized that I could feel so many emotions all at once!

By the time we arrived home, the bouncing game my thoughts were playing had subsided somewhat and my adult/grown-up side had taken over.

Alissa and David took Caitlin out to the pool for a swim, giving Gerry and I a few minutes to talk about the "new" us.

We had already discussed at length, before the doctor's appointment, the fact David may have Asperger's, but, again, the reality of it was still very raw. We made coffee and sat at the kitchen table overlooking the pool where the children were swimming. I could see the same thoughts racing through Gerry's brain, which had been bouncing around mine for the last two hours.

At 8 a.m. on Saturday, January 18, 1997, we had a child who was struggling with some aspects of life. But we had believed that they were developmental and that he would eventually grow out of it, and we "thought" he might have this thing called Asperger's. But at 3 p.m., on Saturday, January 18, 1997, we had a child with Asperger's syndrome. The words were permanently apart of his life, and our lives, forever.

While we were sitting at the kitchen table, both locked in a silent struggle to find the words to make sense of the emotions we were both feeling, David and Alissa were teaching Caitlin how to play Marco Polo in the swimming pool, as if nothing had changed.

Conflicting thoughts were running through our brains. "Marco!" "Polo!" *Splash.* This wasn't temporary; this was permanent. "Marco!" "Polo!" *Splash.* Asperger's syndrome is part of our lives now. "Marco!" "Polo!" *Splash.*

92

I hated it, I hated the word, and I hated the sound of the word. I hated the ramifications and I hated who it had made me, and us, become.

"Marco!" "Polo!" *Splash.* But as much as I hated the words, it was also a step forward for us. The term *Asperger's syndrome* was going to give us the tools, the knowledge, and the skills to move forward. Those words were what we had been searching for and now we had the answer. Now we had a place to start. "Marco!" "Polo!" *Splash.*

I wanted to be angry, but I wasn't. I wanted to cry, but I couldn't. I wanted to be sad, but I was feeling empowered.

After what seemed like an eternity Gerry said, "I think I need a drink."

"Me too!" I replied, perhaps a little too emphatically. So he poured two gin and tonics and we went outside to sit on the steps by the pool. We sat, talking a bit, but for the most part, both of us lost in thought (and trying to avoid getting wet!)

As we each tried to come to terms with the term *Asperger's syndrome* and what that strange two-word phrase now meant for us in our lives, the words "Marco!" and "Polo!" followed by splashing and laughter, dominated the eerie afternoon silence.

Soon the sun would set. Soon we would have to start dinner. Soon we would sit around the table as a family, have dinner, and talk about things we always talk about. But right now, for the moment, while the world was still turning, while the children were playing in the pool, we were trying to come to terms with what the words Asperger's syndrome meant to our lives and how on Saturday, January 18, 1997, our world changed forever.

THE MEDICATION JOURNEY

Wednesday, January 22, 1997

We started David on dextroamphetamine on Sunday. What a difference.

He was animated, his eyes looked different, and he looked straight at you as though he was actually seeing us for the first time. He followed Gerry around all day asking questions about computers. He pulled out the old Amiga computer from under the desk and took it into his room and began to try to fix it, undoing the screws at the back and placing them all in a box.

That night he spent an hour at the table talking to Gerry and he was alive! Unfortunately, he couldn't sleep until 1:30 a.m.

So Monday we gave him two tablets in the morning and a half tablet at 2 p.m. He was still asking questions and talking about computers. At around 2:30 p.m., Gerry said, "Now how do we turn him off?" Unfortunately he couldn't sleep again, although this time it was 10:30 before he finally closed his eyes and he only ate very little dinner.

Tuesday he was very tired. We gave him two tablets in the morning. The kids went to see a movie. He was very quiet when he got in the car and lay down in his bed for an hour. I don't think he slept.

We didn't give him any medication that afternoon and he was back wandering around the tree at 4 p.m.

The trade off seems to be giving him the medication and no sleep or dealing with a rollercoaster. I love having him with us—alive and asking questions. We will just give him two today and see what happens and maybe go back to half tomorrow afternoon before swimming.

I prepared a report for the school principal for the teacher's in-service day; it was difficult to get it down to five pages!

Sunday, January 26, 1997

This week has been an emotional roller coaster. One minute, I feel I am coping well with David's diagnosis, and the next, I crumble in a heap. I thought the diagnosis would make this all different. But one minute, I can be very adult and together about it and feel I can cope with whatever comes, but then something minor will happen and I feel as if the whole world is closing in.

I just lost it after a conversation with Gerry about something very minor. All the pain and hurt I was feeling about David came to the surface. I feel angry and guilty I didn't figure this out earlier; I think I knew…I just didn't want *to know! I wish Mum was still alive. I want to be mothered for a while. I want to just stop being a grown-up. I want somebody to take the responsibility away from me. Just for one day I just don't want to get out of bed. I want somebody to tuck me in, hold me, and tell me it's all going to be ok. Then I will get up the next day and everything will be ok again. Some days I seem to grasp this, understand what's going on and feel so sure of this diagnosis; then the next day something will happen and I realize I don't know enough; I haven't got a grip on this or me! I think I am really nervous and concerned about him starting school this year. I just don't want to be nervous or concerned. I want to be confident and cool and happy David is going back to school, like every other parent. This is so tiring.*

Friday, January 31, 1997

It's been a very busy two days, with getting David settled as well as organizing a Parent's Welcome morning at the school. I still haven't been up to see Alissa's teacher. Poor Alissa was just left on Tuesday to fend for herself. I think she has become used to being independent, way too early really!

Well, David is showing a marked improvement in his work from last year. He worked on a science experiment and actually completed all the observations.

They had to do a 1996 reflection sheet; he answered all the questions well. But I had to chuckle at one of the questions …When asked what he would like to change about Year 6 he responded:

"I wouldn't like to change anything about Year 6. One year in Year 6 is more than enough for me thanks!!"

Gerry and I could not get over the difference in him, in such a short period of time. It felt like we had our son back. Perhaps the medication was the answer and all the worry was in vain. I started to feel more confident and relaxed.

That week at school, everybody noticed a difference, and many teachers wrote notes in his diary or stopped me in the schoolyard to comment: "David is much quieter and more focused in class." "David actually took direction today and stayed on task." "David actually sat still today."

Hallelujah, break out the champagne and fireworks—he is cured!!

Each day, David would take two tablets in the morning and a half tablet in the afternoon, and for the first time in a long time, I actually started to smile. Perhaps this was the answer we were looking for. How wrong I was!

LEARNING MORE ABOUT ASPERGER'S SYNDROME

Over the next few months, we attended as many information sessions and seminars on Asperger's syndrome as we could.

My journal entry from Wednesday, February 12, 1997, describes the outcome of one of the sessions.

Gerry and I attended the parent workshop at the Autistic Society yesterday; it was great to meet other parents and exchange experiences.

So many realizations. ASD kids have trouble with sensory messages. They often don't register hot or cold—David often goes to school with his sweater on and doesn't take it off as it gets warm.

ASD kids are often not aware of their body. This reminded me of the time I asked David where his shoes were. He looked down at his feet and appeared surprised they were not there.

Making sure you tell him what to do, then what to do next. I often send David on an errand to get something from his room, only to find him ten minutes later, standing in his room, with whatever item I have asked him to get but not knowing what to do next.

I found the session empowering; Gerry found it overwhelming. I guess this is the way it will be...Ups and downs all the time.

We had the Child Study meeting with all those involved with David's case on Monday and will get the results today or tomorrow.

During this time, I was also developing and teaching fitness and weight loss seminars and writing a book at the same time. I look back on these journal entries now and just wonder how on earth we got through it, but we did. It was a massive, steep learning curve with many moments of dark and intense questioning and doubt.

Friday, February 14, 1997

What a week! It has been so hot and humid every day.

It's not yet 5:15 a.m. and the humidity is unbearable. The kids are all having trouble sleeping—especially David. He was still awake at 10 p.m. last night. We let him sleep yesterday morning, taking him to school at morning break and that seemed to help him at school for the rest of the day. His teacher said he had been really "spacey" the day before. This seems to be the pattern during the hot weather.

We went to the second workshop last night on Adolescence. There were only two other parents there—the "I know it all, it's worse for me" mother and a lovely lady from the country.

I learned some great distinctions. Adolescence is a more positive time for ASD children, as they often become more motivated to learn about making friends. Last night we took his friend Mark to training and David asked him "social questions." He just didn't know what to do with the answers, but at least it is a big step forward for him.

I noticed one of the mothers used the word problem *all the time. "He understands he has a problem." I don't see this as a problem; I see it as a difference. David seems to be more caring*

100

than what I have come to learn about ASD kids and has a deeper understanding of world issues. He and Alissa both seem, at this stage, to be very insightful .... I would like to think it comes from their upbringing!

Tuesday, February 18, 1997

David came home yesterday very tired and very spacey. Couldn't get him to do his homework. It was like David in the old days. I am more than concerned about him going to high school. I am not really sure if he is going to be able to cope with the workload.

David brought home his family tree, an activity he had to do for school. His was very simple.

Nana Johnston – Deceased

Papa Johnston – Golfer

Gerry Thibault – Father. Does great stuff with me

Sally Thibault – Mother. Thinks she is the maid of the house!!

Wednesday, February 20, 1997

Classic David yesterday.

He got a bee sting on his foot. We put ice on it, but he couldn't concentrate because he was worried about the ice melting. So Gerry gave him a bucket to put his foot in. Five minutes later, Gerry hears a clump, clump *coming up from the bedroom. It's David with his foot in the bucket, walking up to the kitchen to ask him a question!*

He forgot to take his tablet yesterday, and he was back to David of old. Wandering around the tree as soon as he got home from school and it was impossible to try to get him to start on his homework.

A couple of boys from another class started teasing him yesterday, and two boys from his own class alerted his teacher—he says they are very protective of him…Where am I going to find that next year—why didn't we have it last year?

Friday, February 21, 1997

It was parent–teacher night last night. His teacher sounds just so perfect for him. David wrote me a letter and left it in his desk, saying he hoped he would be nominated for class captain!

Alissa's teacher told me she thought Alissa was her brightest student and how lovely she was to have in her class. How nice to just sit and allow those lovely words to just wash over me!

But Alissa was feeling very left out yesterday, so we are going to do something together this week. Between David and Caitlin, there is usually not much time left for Alissa. I am sure she must be feeling it. That's the problem with having a child like her. She never complains and I just automatically assume she is OK. I will look forward to spending some quality time with her, just the two of us together.

Saturday, February 22, 1997

I bought all the staff at school a box of chocolates to thank them for all the work they have done with David. I am very grateful for the way they have embraced this diagnosis and have tried to understand what life is like for him.

However, yesterday afternoon reminded me exactly what life will be like for David from now on.

I was watching some of his friends sauntering through the roundabout area, chatting and bantering together, looking just like Year 7 "big kids." David was totally oblivious (it seemed) to his surroundings. At the same time, he tries so hard to be kind to others, but he doesn't seem to understand the intricate nature of friendships, things that just seem to come so naturally to others. It made me feel so sad.

Tuesday, February 25, 1997

It's hot; the last three days have been almost unbearable. David is not coping at all well in the heat. He is very spacey and very emotional. We have upped his medication to a full tablet in the afternoon, and it makes a bit of a difference. But the trade-off is his inability to sleep, although we all feel like that right now...I feel as if I could sleep for a month!

Thursday, February 27, 1997

I drove up to the workshop yesterday, and after listening to some of the horror stories about some ASD behaviors, I was starting to feel very proud of David.

I am not sure how much of what and who he is can be discerned by Nature vs. Nurture, but some key elements I believe, have been how some people treat this as a problem, rather than a difference, a disaster rather than a challenge. Three women I spoke to yesterday are having real problems with their own emotions in dealing with their children. How much of coping with this diagnosis, for both the parents and the child, is for us, as parents, coming to terms with our own emotions and our own pain?

Monday, March 3, 1997

David told me at 11 p.m. on Friday he had organized to go over to a friend's house on Sunday. He mentioned it again on Saturday night, and at 8 a.m. on Sunday, his friend's mother phoned to say her son had been bugging her all weekend to phone David. I was so excited. He was actually asked to go to somebody's house to play!

He had a great day. He came home tired, but very satisfied. What a different experience for him.

Thursday, March 6, 1997

David has had a tough week.

The class was given a local government project to research. He came home from school and went straight out to the tree. I finally convinced him to come inside and sat with him while we chunked each section down simply. Gerry tried later to do the same thing. You could see the tension and stress building. First in his eyes, then the emotion started to build and the tears started. We had to keep stepping back and continually chunking down the information so it was almost in point form. It took enormous patience, but by the end of it, we were starting to see a bit of a breakthrough.

My goodness, it was taking all of our intuition to keep pulling him back to the assignment so he understood it and not become overwhelmed. It was like we had to anticipate the words he couldn't understand ahead of him actually getting to them and change them into dialogue he could grasp. Breaking everything down so it was very succinct and there was no room for second-guessing.

Thursday, March 11, 1997

Another very stressful night with David's homework.

The local government project may be swamping him. One of the questions last night was how to write a policy speech. He had absolutely no idea where to start. I ended up making it an interview and fed him the answers.

Gerry then spent another hour with him in the office doing the rest of his homework, with many tears. Tutoring for next term may be the answer. It would certainly help the stress levels in our house.

Our meeting with the Education Department representatives today may help shed some light on our option for next year. But at this stage, high school seems like such a huge hurdle to attempt.

Friday, March 12, 1997

We met with the representatives from the Education Department and David's teachers yesterday regarding high schools for next year. Outcome was not the best. There are only a few schools equipped to cope with children with Asperger's or Autistic Spectrum. The words used by the representative were rather chilling. "Actually, we really can't guarantee David's safety, and I am not sure if David will qualify for any assistance, either inside or outside of the classroom."

Patty told me about a new independent school which may be set up enough for him and there are other ASD kids going there; however, a larger school may be a better choice as far as teachers go.

At the same time, we discussed homework. Patty suggested we cut down on his homework considerably. Yesterday, for his English homework, he only did the dictionary meanings, way less than he was supposed to do, and seemed to cope OK. I asked him if his project was worrying him, and he said he wished he could do it every night to get it finished!

After the drama of the night before, tonight he seemed quite settled (remembered to take his tablets). He said he had been to see the counselor today and really liked going to talk to her. He drew a board game for her, and they played it.

He was very excited to find out Gerry would be working for the local government candidate on Election Day. So I said, "Would you like to go with Dad?" His eyes lit up. "I would love to," he said. He was very interested in how Gerry got to work for the candidate. His mood lifted enormously. No tree wandering— he even got the clothes off the line for me.

He came to bed with me and seemed to settle quite early. We did some relaxation and visualization with him and he responded well, becoming very sleepy, very quickly.

Friday, March 14, 1997

David seems much more settled now with the pressure of homework gone. He seems much more alert and sleeping better. He is very keen to get his assignment completed. Maybe the stress of the work was getting to him.

It was so sad watching the sports carnival yesterday.

I watched as the other kids competed, then mucked around together, while David wandered off by himself and didn't seem connect at all with the other boys. He will not experience that comfortable interaction others just take for granted as a part of friendship. Asperger's makes life so lonely.

Tuesday, March 18, 1997

Asperger's reality check! It was the school swimming carnival yesterday.

David stressed out at 8:30 a.m. on the way to school.

We were late and he said he had to have a yellow swimming cap. As he was walking to the bus he was yelling at me, "Mum, I have to have a yellow swim cap." On the way to the carnival, I drove to the school and called into the bookshop, but they had sold out of yellow hats. So I went to the pharmacy and the girl behind the counter sold me a yellow, very expensive, cap for him. I raced back to the pool to find the kids had all colors...David's

teacher had said if *they had a yellow hat, they should wear it....*
He obviously missed the if *part.*

Wednesday, March 19, 1997

I booked David and Alissa into art classes this week. They also tried out for the swimming squad at Southport. David certainly needs the fitness and I think Alissa will enjoy it.

We had to complete the local government project last night. What a night for patience levels! David had to summarize the election speech and had absolutely no idea what the words meant.

As he started to cry, I asked him what was worrying him—he said it was me asking him all the questions. It must frustrate him not to know. Only got to question seven (Gerry taking over in the middle).

After dinner we tackled the collage he had to put together to create a poster. I began cutting things out. He said, "Mum, this is my project; I want to do it my way." He then stood at the kitchen table from 7:30 till 9 putting together the collage.

After dinner last night, it was so cute. Caitlin, Alissa and David started dancing to the Macarena. Alissa and Caitlin just flowed with the music, adding different moves. David was almost, but not quite, half a beat behind, although managing to keep time, as he was actually listening to the music and then doing the action. It must have been very difficult for him to do the dance, and yet a couple of times, when the phrase changed, he knew when to stop and how to pick the beat back up again.

Maybe we have been looking at this incorrectly? Maybe he needs more creative work, music lessons, art, acting, and he seemed to enjoy the musical they did at school. Unfortunately, his speech lets him down, but his memory is amazing. He knows everybody else's lines and fills in for anybody who is away. However, I think he may always be relegated to minor roles as his ability to interact with others is so limited.

THE LIGHT BULB MOMENT

I didn't realize it at the time, but journaling during this time helped me find solutions. Or rather perhaps it enabled me to get the thoughts out of my "bouncing" brain and to make some sense of the emotions I was feeling.

Friday, March 21, was, what I believe, a "light bulb moment," the stage I finally needed to get to, in order to truly understand what my (our) role was in David's life.

Friday, March 21, 1997

I attended an ASD support group meeting yesterday with guest speakers. During the meeting, many mothers expressed their frustration at not being able to access services for their children.

Memories came flooding back of the hours spent at speech and occupational therapy; the hours talking to teachers and seeking information from many different sources that went on in the early days before David's diagnosis. I remembered how much we were on our own; how much time, effort, patience, learning, anger, sorrow and despair we felt. I remembered not wanting to go anywhere because of what he might do. And if we did go somewhere, then spending the hours later with him trying to get him to understand why certain things were not acceptable.

Two things I realized today:

Perhaps it was a blessing we didn't know about Asperger's in the early years. Perhaps it made us search longer and harder for solutions. Perhaps we intuitively knew in order for us to cope with this, we had to figure out who we were in order to deal with this effectively, and really it hasn't been such a bad thing.

I also see ASD as being as much about the parents as it is about the child. Because every conceivable belief and thought you have about who you are as a parent and what role you play in the whole parenting thing are challenged.

As I was driving home yesterday, it suddenly dawned on me why we have done all the things we have. The personal development seminars, books, long discussions about our beliefs, emotions etc. Taking responsibility for ourselves is imperative before we could deal effectively with this diagnosis. We have to accept our role as the primary caregiver; be willing to let go of expectations and accept David as a whole being, different in a world which doesn't accept differences well; and being willing to change our beliefs, our attitudes, and our plans at any point.

Having an ASD child forces you to not only look at just who you really are but also what your expectations are of and for your child.

ASD children are different, but they are also connected to a source different from our own. Their ability to concentrate, to remain self-focused, even their inability to socialize needs to be seen as strengths.

Socialization is society's way of measuring acceptance and normalcy. Being normal is the handicap; being different is the freedom!

It is our role as David's parents to accept, acknowledge, and grow with this difference; to discover his talents and foster these; to allow his difference to be his strength. But most of all, to accept the differences and allow him to create his own expectations and capabilities.

This is not our life—this is David's life. We can't measure his life by what he cannot do; instead, we must focus on what he can bring to the world. Constant fostering and encouragement of his interests will find a solution no one else will find.

It was the beginning of the change. Once I had made my mind up to look at this differently, things began to change.

I began to question the medication and, although it solved some issues in the short term, was it really going to work in the long term? Dextroamphetamine, although kept him focused and less distracted, was also making him somebody he was not. He wasn't our son while he was taking it. It was making him like a robot. Compliant, quiet, and submissive. Willing to sit still at his desk at school—but it wasn't making him normal. It wasn't helping him understand emotion, either his or anybody else's. Was this what I truly wanted for my son? One minute, he was up; next minute, he was down. Sometimes the medication seemed to work; other times, it didn't. It was like walking a very thin tightrope. I felt I was losing him, but I didn't know the other answer—yet!

Monday, March 24, 1997

David didn't have any medication yesterday, and there appeared to be no difference in his behaviors. He spent Saturday at a friend's house, didn't say much about it, although seemed to enjoy the day.

Friday, March 28, 1997

I had a very positive meeting yesterday with David's support teachers. David's work has improved a great deal. He is motivated in class and determined to do the same work as the other kids, especially in science and math. Even his comprehension is improving. At least he is willing to try to read and comprehend.

His teacher told me today he stood up in front of the class and presented his election speech without palm cards and did the whole thing from memory—she congratulated me on working with him on it. I knew he had to write one, but I didn't know he had to present it. He amazes me sometimes.

Patty gave me some books for him to read at home, to see if we can get him interested in reading...he read two of them last night. I had just left them sitting on his bed.

He was obviously feeling very good about himself last night. I asked him what was different about this year to last, and he said the tablets made it easier for him to concentrate. I also feel it is us being more aware of his stress levels (thank God I had a diagnosis before we started on the assignment; otherwise, I would have strangled him!).

Even his social skills seem to be improving. Last night at dinner, he asked, "So what are you guys doing tomorrow—are you working in the office?" I thought he was asking the question because he wanted us to do something...he said, "No, I just wanted to know." OK, so just when I think I should take him off the medication, he has a good week while on it. Good grief, this is hard work.

Friday, April 4, 1997

I met a nice lady today who was telling me about a friend of hers who had a son with Asperger's. I was under the impression he was a lovely boy, but she says he has a very explosive temper, swears all the time, lashes out at his mum, and steals.

This seems to be a very common trait among ASD boys, I wonder if it is hormonal? Or the downside to depression, I wonder if they are always like this, or does their demeanor change during adolescence? David hasn't reached that stage yet—is it something to look forward to?

Saturday, April 19, 1997

An up-and-down week. David seems very anxious and stressed this week and was bursting into tears a lot. The doctor has prescribed Zoloft to help with the anxiety. After reading about it, I am a little concerned about putting him on it. There seems to be quite a few side effects, but he can't continue like this. I really feel for him.

Patty recommended David see the school counselor who could perhaps help him deal with the anxiety and create strategies to help him at school.

Sister Ann is a lovely nun with a beautiful smiling face and a quick and funny sense of humor. David loved going to see her because she let him draw and didn't ask too many questions all the time!

Tuesday, April 22, 1997

David saw Sister Ann yesterday. Hard to know how it went, although he was very helpful with Caitlin last night and very attentive at swimming. He really lit up when I thanked him for his help.

He was also very excited. He had been given the task of looking after the Jokes section in the class newsletter. He wants to belong and feel a sense of involvement with his peers. This gives him something tangible to be a part of...perfect.

Alissa was very upset when she got in the car this afternoon and wouldn't talk for ages. I finally asked her what was wrong. She said she had seen some Grade Six boys making fun of David. It really upset her.

Wednesday, April 30, 1997

David seems less anxious about things this week, although the trade-off seems to be he is very quiet and almost spacey again.

Something I realized after watching an interview with Tiger Woods and his dad was even though David is different from others; we must ensure it does not become a handicap!

ALARM BELLS—
TIME FOR CHANGE

My doubts about keeping David on medication were answered loud and clear one morning the following week. I called David to come for breakfast. I had his medication ready. He walked into the kitchen, one sock on and one sock in his hand, and said, "Mum, I don't know what to do next." Alarm bells rang loud and clear; this was not working. Something needed to change.

Being a parent is hard. Being a parent of a handsome, loving, funny child with a difference that appears to be "simply a matter of discipline and behavior" is heartbreaking. This was no longer about listening to all the medical expertise, the educational expertise, the opinions and thoughts of others. I was this child's mother. I knew him better than anybody else did. I decided that I needed to become the expert in understanding how Asperger's affected his life. I needed to stay focused on what was best for my child to ensure that the decisions made were the best for David at the time, based on what I believed to be true, not because others told me what to do.

I decided that I was going to gain as much knowledge as I could about Asperger's, then make decisions with my heart.

But first he needed to be whole and medication was not going to allow him to be that. He couldn't grow, learn, and genuinely experience love, if his medication stopped him from feeling emotion. Sure it was fine for the quick fix; sure it helped him sit at a desk and be compliant; but it wasn't giving him the skills he would need throughout his life. How would he ever understand his emotions, if he wasn't given the opportunity to discover them now? At some point he was going to have to learn how to deal with anger, stress or frustration without medication. But if he didn't do it now, while he was surrounded by his parents and those who loved him so that he had a safety net to fall back on, then when was he going to figure them out? One thing I did know for sure, those diagnosed with Asperger's needed to learn all the things in life that neurotypical people just take for granted, being able to deal effectively with emotion was one of those things.

If we were going to move ahead with this, I needed him whole and present and I needed to be whole and present. I also had a feeling that while this all made sense in my head, putting this all into our physical reality may be challenging. I needed to wean him off his medication gradually and then start the long process of helping him create strategies that could help him deal with any emotion he was feeling. I knew in my heart, that deciding to teach David to navigate life without medication was going to be tough and it would be a long journey. At the time I didn't realize how tough or how long it would actually be, but once I made my mind up there was no going back.

Friday, May 2, 1997

David's teacher stopped me Wednesday to say David was totally off the planet—unable to complete even simple tasks.

I phoned the doctor and took him straight off Zoloft. Yesterday, David's teacher saw me after school again and said there had been a marked improvement in his work and attitude. He seemed to be thinking clearly. I feel he must metabolize drugs very quickly to have a very fast reaction. Even he said not taking the tablet helped his mind to think better. But the trade-off is he can't sleep and becomes more anxious when just on the dex.

114

I have made an appointment with a doctor who deals in natural therapies for next week. I think we need to research that avenue now.

Wednesday, May 14, 1997

David's anxiety levels are high again. At the Art Gallery on Sunday, he thought we were in the wrong place and got very upset. Later that night, he couldn't understand why you work hard at school to enjoy weekends, and then got upset because Gerry didn't know who discovered the planets!

Had an appointment with the natural therapies doctor yesterday, $187 later and a concoction of vitamins—B6, magnesium, zinc, evening primrose oil, fish oil and one to help him sleep. He said about three weeks before they begin to work. He is going to order some DMG from the States, I phoned Department of Social Security enquiring about the Disability allowance— treating David naturally will cost us a fortune!

And so began the slow process of weaning David off the medication and focusing totally on using natural therapies. DMG, or dimethylglycine, is a form of the amino acid glycine and has been used with some success in improving neurological function. The first of many natural therapies we attempted over the years!

Monday, July 14, 1997

The DMG is certainly making David chattier and a bit easier to deal with. His teacher said on Thursday he was sticking to tasks a lot better this term already.

Friday, July 24, 1997

DMG is working well with David. He is down to half a tablet of Dex, and says he feels much better. At Taekwondo last week, he organized a game of helicopters with the older boys. He seems be more "normal" now, talking about a lot of different things. I will order more B6/magnesium today and get him started on that straight away.

Friday, August 8, 1997

More tears with David. He is not feeling like these new tablets are doing anything. I think he is missing the "buzz" as there

appears to be no problem with his abilities—not like last year.
But I have a feeling he may be adjusting to the difference.

David began preparing for a school trip to Canberra. The bus trip would take them on a tour of the Capital, to visit a session of parliament and then to the snow, where he was going to go ski-ing for the very first time. He was very excited.

Thursday, August 28, 1997

The countdown begins to the Canberra trip. David is so excited, as are all the Year 7's. What a wonderful experience for them all and what a lovely class of kids. I love seeing David so excited. He is animated and talkative and involved in what is going on. It's as if the excitement turns on an "I'm here!" button for him.

Monday, September 1, 1997

David left last night for Canberra. Great excitement all round. Although marked with a little sadness as most of the talk among the parents was the death of Princess Diana in Paris.

After spending so much time at the school with David, I was offered a position as a part-time teacher's aide working in the special education unit. It came as a complete surprise but was a role I knew I would enjoy immensely.

Friday 5 September 1997

I started work at the school this week as a teacher's aide. At first I was hesitant to take on the role while trying to get the book to print, but I had made a conscious decision last week; not to turn down any work "in case" something else comes along. I believe this was sent at the right time. Even though it is hard work to balance everything, I am enjoying it.

Monday, September 8, 1997

David arrived home at 8:30 Friday night very tired and saved his last camera shot to take a photo of us as he got off the bus.

He was very affectionate, loved the snow, but didn't like being with the kids all the time and hated sleeping with everyone around him. First thing Saturday morning he was around the tree. He is so very different.

The principal stopped me at the Family Fun day and asked how I had enjoyed teaching this week. And I had to answer her truthfully. I really enjoyed it and felt a sense of purpose working with these kids. I really feel so much of it is because of having to deal with David for all these years. She suggested starting a parent support group for those with different children…no argument here!

During this time, we began earnestly looking for high schools for David. This was a new era for us and one I was very concerned about.

It had taken a long time for David to be accepted into the school environment. How was he going to adjust to a new school at the time of his life when puberty was kicking in? Just when I thought things couldn't get any more stressful, they did.

I also commenced my Diploma in Professional Counseling. I had wanted to study counseling for many years and kept putting it off. The assignments and study were challenging, but I enjoyed learning more about why people do what they do!

ASCERTAINMENT TIME

In order to ascertain David's needs for high school, we were required to undergo an "Ascertainment." We, together with his teachers, were required to respond to a series of questions, present medical and specialist reports to a panel, who then decided whether David was eligible for funding to receive assistance to help him once he entered high school.

Thursday, September 18, 1997

Spring Carnival for the day care center! I ran the second-hand clothing store, and David took the role as the promoter for the chocolate wheel, encouraging people to buy tickets to win prizes. He did a wonderful job. The difference in him when he was on the microphone to when he wasn't was simply amazing. He seems to become someone else when he is on stage, as long as he doesn't have to be involved in a conversation.

David's Ascertainment on Tuesday. What a farce! Ascertained at Level Four—no facilities or services available for him in any state high school.

Thank goodness we have a choice. We will have a choice. I will make it my choice. I will move heaven and earth to get my child the best schooling available. This whole process makes me angry, sad, and frustrated and at the same time just plain thankful we have had the help we have had until now. I know by listening to my heart that I will find the right thing for David; I just have to keep looking and asking for it.

That afternoon I contacted the new independent school that Patty had suggested, and made an appointment to take David out there the next week.

Monday morning at nine Gerry, David, and I took the long trek out to see the school. It was about a forty-five-minute one-way trip and at the time we didn't have air-conditioning in our car. All I could think was we only have one car! How on earth am I going to drop Gerry at work, two children at two different schools and Caitlin at day care every single morning with only one car? Well, if it was right, we would find a solution somehow.

Our introduction to the headmaster was something I had never experienced before. It was as though we were invisible. He spoke to David for the entire thirty minutes, and David replied with sometimes-relevant-to-the-question answers.

He then took us on a tour around the school, and after an hour, we left.

The question didn't have to be asked; it hung between Gerry and me: How on earth can we afford this?' However, as we drove down the long, bumpy drive, we both had the same feeling: if we moved David out to this school, our lives would change. The prediction was absolutely correct.

Monday, September 29, 1997

David was very spaced out all weekend. I was lucky enough to meet a lady on the weekend who did her thesis on Asperger's syndrome. She was very informative and her expertise gave me an opportunity to understand how David would be if his diagnosis had not been made when it was.

Thursday, October 2, 1997

David stayed the night at a friend's, who actually asked him to stay. David was thrilled. We then met up at the environmental park for a picnic with the family. He was very interactive with all the kids there and seemed to be having a great time.

While I worked at the school, I was introduced to a young psychology student from a local University. She had come to the school to talk about a new research project they were starting, designed to help anxious kids create strategies to cope with life. I thought it would be perfect for David, and although he didn't totally fit the criteria, I convinced her that he would benefit. Never under estimate the power of a mother's persuasion skills!

Tuesday, October 8, 1997

We drove to Brisbane last night in the pouring rain to take David for his interview. It was a long interview and, at first, I felt they were not going to take him, but we talked our way into the program. Gerry and I both felt that he would benefit from a program such as this, so we had to use all our persuasion skills to ensure he was included.

David was lovely on the way up. He really enjoyed just being with Gerry and I and very chatty and funny. He read to us his poem and his story he is doing for the speech exam, and he was very funny.

It was busy at school today. I finally got agreement to start a social skills program. David came down at lunchtime to start work on his journal. He just kept touching me and smiling with a sigh. I'm not sure if it is because he now has something to do at lunchtime or because I am there. It doesn't seem to worry him that I am; he is so different from other kids.

Saturday, October 11, 1997

David has been very stressed this week. He had an altercation with his swim coach on Wednesday and David kicked him. David was adamant that he was unfairly treated and does not want to go back.

He has been very stressed at school and retaliating toward other kids, where before he would ignore them. He has also been very teary at home. At this stage, we are putting it down to his anticipation of beginning high school and having to leave his school. We put in an application for review of his ascertainment to see if there is any funding available for him next year.

Sometimes I feel totally overwhelmed. I have started David on St. John's Wort to see if that helps with his anxiety. I think I need to start on it too!

Monday, October 14, 1997

David has been much better this week after starting on St. John's Wort; Gerry has been taking it as well and says he feels better. However, David had a fight with his friend today and is feeling very stressed about it. One step forward... two steps back!

Thursday, October 23, 1997

David was awarded the Good Behavior award this week. He was very pleased with himself. He just missed out on getting the part of Elvis in the end-of-school concert. Anyway, he seemed pleased most of the kids thought he should have gotten the part.

Friday, October 24, 1997

The school had a visit from an advisor from the Autism Society yesterday to observe David. She felt he has very high needs and is very stressed. She will write a good letter for the ascertainment. I am really concerned for next year for him. Patty said she would come out to the new school to brief his teachers.

Monday, October 27, 1997

Great weekend. Friends of ours had asked us to meet them at the beach where their children were involved in the local Nippers Surf Lifesaving Club. In a momentary loss of sanity, I asked David if he would like to try out for Nippers. "Sure!" he said. "Alissa, do you want to do it too?" Great, another activity, another commitment, more money to find!

Friday, December 5, 1997

Well, today is the final day of life at primary school. The graduation mass was beautiful. David had to bring a special letter he wasn't allowed to tell anybody about, especially Gerry and me. I read the note in his bag, which listed all the things he was supposed to do. When I questioned him about the sentence, "Don't forget your special letter," he replied, "Oh, that was from last year."

He kept it secret all night, until the principal told the students to give their special letter to their parents. It was just lovely.

122

The graduation dinner went well, and the kids had a great time. David took a while to figure it all out, but after a couple of hours, he got involved. He even danced the progressive jive with a smile on his face!

By the end of the year, I was physically and emotionally exhausted. It had been a big year, but we had a diagnosis and we had options for David. We were one step further along than we were the year before, and it had been a big year of change and learning for our family.

What I didn't realize was that this journey had only just begun.

HIGH SCHOOL

Year 8, 1998; the beginning of a whole new world.

David was still a small child with a very fine build, dark olive skin, and light brown hair often bleached blond by the summer sun. He was a very good-looking boy, which was, of course, one of the issues we constantly had to deal with. He looked so "normal."

People would often question whether we were using the label of Asperger's syndrome as an excuse for his behavior. He could look and present in a very neurotypical way. Only when he was asked to answer a question, or tried to interact socially, or was placed in noisy stressful situations did his difference became obvious. Even so, his reactions were still often judged as bad or inappropriate behavior, because most people had little understanding of what Asperger's syndrome really was.

He looked too young to be entering high school and we were both very nervous, not only about starting a new school but also about how he would cope with the changes from his familiar primary school to a place where he had to start all over again and where nobody knew him.

After spending hours on the Internet researching more information about Asperger's syndrome, I prepared a detailed report for the school, aimed at assisting the staff to understand his diagnosis. *(This report is now available on our Web site www. davidsgift.com.au, and I welcome you to use it to help staff at*

125

school develop appropriate strategies unique to your child and when preparing or reviewing your child's IEP). I also gave the report to my family and friends so they could also understand why David sometimes reacted the way he did.

We had numerous meetings with the head of the high school and David's tutorial teacher. As a relatively new school, the high school was very small, and we thought this would suit David because people would perhaps get to know him.

The teachers created colored copies of David's timetable: one to put in his diary, one to put in his locker, one to put in his room at home, and one for me. We visited the school a number of times before the first day of school, so he got used to where his locker would be, what the bell sounded like, where different rooms were, and where the toilets and changing rooms were.

Preparation for the change seemed to be going well. Throughout the weeks leading up to the beginning of school, David appeared to be coping well with any anxiety, although as the time drew closer we began to see changes in his behavior.

Saturday, January 10, 1998

David has been off his medication all of the holidays and has had good days and bad days. Of course, the stress of school is not present, and he certainly doesn't appear to be as vague as he usually is. Once we get some more money, I will send away for more DMG, B6, and magnesium. And put him back onto St. John's Wort for a week before school so he is not stressed.

Saturday, January 17, 1998

We had a friend over on Wednesday night, not a great success. David was more interested in playing Nintendo than playing with his friend—and his friend was more interested in playing in the pool with Alissa and Caitlin.

Monday, January 19, 1998

We had a classic 'David' moment at Nippers yesterday. Gerry told David to put his goggles on top of his head while he was racing in the beach race. After the race was finished, he then ran all the way up the beach to ask, "Dad, can I please have my goggles back?" They were sitting on top of his head.

Monday, January 26, 1998

David is very stressed about going to a new school. I thought he would be OK on Saturday after we went out and got all his uniforms and books, but it only seemed to make him worse. We found the class list last night, and it seemed to settle him. He at least knew some of the other boys who would be in the same class. There are only twenty-three kids in the class altogether, so at least it is a small class to start with.

Tuesday, January 27, 1998

We had a lovely day yesterday. We spent an hour in the pool—Gerry and David had a "rumble" in the pool, and David really connected with him. We all watched the cricket game that was televised that night, and when it was over, David said, "You can go to bed now, Mum." He really wanted to spend time with Gerry alone.

A New Era, a New Set of Challenges

The time had come, and the next era was about to begin. Gerry and I had discussed at length the issue about Alissa and David being a different school. In the end, we decided for everybody's sanity that it would be best if she was at the same school as David. At least that meant one less drop-off every morning. Our decision was made very easy when Alissa was offered a scholarship to commence at the same time as David, making the impact on our budget a little easier.

So with new uniforms and great expectations, both David and Alissa started at the new school, with a student orientation day. For both of the children this was nerve-racking, but for David even more so. We had rehearsed with David some of the questions he could ask other children. "Hello, my name is David. What's your name?" "Hello, this is my first day at this school. Is it your first day?" were just some of the questions we had practiced.

He concentrated and drew on all his confidence to walk up to others to create conversations; it's just after he got past those questions, he had no idea how to continue the conversation and the other kids, sensing something different, just ignored him anyway. However, it was a start.

Those with Asperger's syndrome can be so confusing to understand. They often have moments of brilliance and complete normalcy that tend to throw you off guard and think perhaps that this "difference" is just a figment of your imagination.

The first two weeks seemed fine. He was happy and inter-active, talked a little on the way home about his new teachers and who was kind and who wasn't—a very important aspect in David's world. Kind people were usually gentle and understand-ing, naturally knowing how to converse with him. Those who were not kind were people who demanded too much, asked too many questions, or insisted on him conforming to their demands.

Monday, February 9, 1998

It has been a busy, fulfilling, and exciting week. David and Alissa appear to have settled into the new school.

At the Parent Information night, every teacher, without exception, said David was enthusiastic and happy in class. One teacher even said, "If you hadn't given us that report, we would not have known there is anything different about him."

I thought for a split second that perhaps I was over-exag-gerating —perhaps David was growing out of his "Asperger's syndrome." Perhaps I was being an over protective mother. It didn't take long for me to be thrown back into reality!

It's All about to Change

It was the third week that bought the dream run to a nerve-shattering end. In the midsession of one particular morning, there was a change in rooms announced at tutorial group. The tutorial teacher read out the notices and saw David was looking at him so assumed he understood.

So at 9:40, just before the start of the second period, David went to get his math books and walked into the classroom where math normally took place. He just walked in and sat down, not realizing that he was in the Year 10 English class. All the kids laughed at him.

He looked up and only saw a strange teacher and unfamiliar kids all laughing at him. In an instant, all the progress he had made in the first two weeks was gone. He panicked, picked up his books, rushed outside, and stood outside the classroom and cried.

One of the other teachers saw him and took him down to the school office to see the head of the high school. David couldn't explain what had happened and couldn't understand why things had changed. From then on, the bad days got worse and the good days became fewer and farther between.

High school is different. Students are expected to become more organized, more self-sufficient, and more able to navigate the complicated room-numbering systems, bells, and changes to routine. Allowances were made in the first few weeks, but after that, students were expected to become more independent. However, David couldn't. While other students became more adept at the freedom of high school, David became more agitated and began to retreat into himself. He hated changing classroom after each period. He would often get lost because the stress from the noise and the movement of the other students, laughing and playing around, caused a great deal of concern for him. He was often late for class, which would then make him even more anxious. And if he was asked by the teacher why he was late, he often couldn't answer because he couldn't find the words to respond appropriately. This would then result in yet another discipline—usually standing outside the classroom. He had no idea why he was made to stand outside, and that again added to his stress levels even further.

Not long after school started, all the Year 8 students attended a five day long camp, designed to help them get to know each other. Accompanied by teachers, the camp involved lots of different activities, such as canoeing and swimming. David normally loved school camps, however as his stress levels were beginning to increase, I was concerned that he may find the week away very difficult.

Saturday, February 28, 1998

David came back from camp yesterday. I am not sure how it really went as I received some very cryptic and noncommittal comments from the teachers. His differences are becoming more pronounced now, and he is retreating into his own world. I know he is also going through puberty, and it is normal for boys to have one word answers...however, I think his are one word answers because he doesn't know any other words to respond with.

So the New Challenges Continue

I was often called up to the school. "David loses pencils, pens, socks, books." "He is constantly disorganized." "He comes to class unprepared." "He is often more than five minutes late for class." "He seems as if he doesn't understand the questions I ask."

We continually met with teachers, going over lesson plans, behavior plans, and academic plans and continually coming up with new solutions, creating new options.

Twice a week, the students were expected to participate in a sports program. At the school he attended, the students were expected to wear their day school uniform to school, change into their school sporting uniform for the class, and change back into their day uniform at the end of school. This was a particularly stressful process for David. He hated getting changed in the locker rooms before sport. They were smelly, noisy, and the boys were constantly pushing and shoving or yelling when they were getting changed. He dreaded going into the locker rooms and would become noticeably more and more anxious as sport days loomed. Besides, he wasn't very good at ball sports and was often relegated to the worst team with others who hated sport as well. So for him, there was no reasonable reason to both change into the sports uniform and actually participate in sport. Once David had made his mind up whether something was reasonable or understandable or not, there was usually no going back. Packing his sports uniform into his schoolbag then became a stressful event in itself.

We felt perhaps if we could remove the major cause of his anxiety, which was changing into his sports uniform, then participating in sport would not be such an issue for him. We debated for weeks with the teachers to try to get them to allow David to come to school, on sports days, in his sports uniform. Finally, after yet another pushing, shoving, and yelling incident in the locker rooms, David was finally grated a dispensation to come to school in his sports uniform on sports days. While this was a good outcome, during the process of debating this issue, life was slowly spiraling downward.

Year 8was a constant challenge, some days good, some days dreadful. I had to constantly ask myself the question, is this Asperger's we are dealing with, or is this puberty? I didn't want to get the two mixed up. Some things David did and went through were perfectly normal for a twelve-year-old boy, and some things were not. Trying to figure out which was which was making my head hurt!

Tuesday, March 10, 1998

I had a meeting with David's teachers today. David is not coping well in the subjects with a lot of words. I phoned Patty to get David's IEP (Individualized Education Plan) from last year, especially for English and Studies of Society and Environment. And after last week's incident, they have agreed to set him up with a buddy.

In the week prior to the meeting, there had been an accident on the motorway, and due to traffic hold-ups, it took me two hours to get to school to pick him up. Alissa had been home sick on the day, and with her not being at school, I was very concerned because I knew David would be worried. But I assumed the teachers, or somebody, would have advised him. But as it turned out, nobody did, and he waited at the school gate for two hours … nobody noticed. I was devastated and he was distraught. He needed somebody to notice him!

Tuesday, March 17, 1998

David was very happy last night. He got to meet the man who invented the computer in 1948 and have his picture taken with him, which will be in the local newspaper. He felt very proud of himself. He also played chess at lunchtime and beat Alissa!

Saturday, April 25, 1998

David is certainly growing up. He said last night, "The work is really tough—but I am trying my best." However, he did get stressed when his science homework wasn't right. The teacher asked him to do something that wasn't in the book!

Tuesday, April 28, 1998

David was very happy and talkative today. Last night he was working on his math homework, a project with a complicated math problem. After a number of attempts he figured it out and felt very proud of himself. He was having so much fun with it and then came out and asked me for something to help him sleep as he was getting worried about not waking up in the morning. He asked if I would splash cold water on his face!

Thursday, May 21, 1998

It has been so long since I wrote in this journal. But I wanted to remember Mother's Day.

All week there had been whispering behind closed doors. Then on Sunday morning, Alissa and Caitlin woke me up with their presents. Alissa and David made a book they had created of a collage of all our family photos. The time, effort, and love to create this book was obvious. I was overwhelmed. Caitlin bought me a coffee cup, decorated with hearts, but full of lollipops—she couldn't wait for me to open up the wrapping.

Then they all got dressed up in their nicest clothes, and we went out for breakfast. During breakfast, David was freezing. I asked him if he would like to move inside. He said, "It's your Mother's Day, Mum, and I know you want to sit outside...I'll be fine." What a gorgeous kid!

Monday, June 8, 1998

My baby is thirteen. I remember the day he was born as if it was yesterday. Yes, he is so different from the other kids, but he is also a great kid, with some nice friends.

He had five friends he wanted to come over for his birthday. They all came over on Saturday about five and played Nintendo. Then they played football in the backyard and ate tons of pizza and watched videos. On Sunday they all went to Intensity, a computer gaming place, for two hours and loved it.

Wednesday, June 17, 1998

School reports arrived. David's wasn't bad. He attained a B for Math, and a C+ for Indonesian, Physical Education, and Studies of Society and Environment, but failed computers and art, which was surprising. But considering he did little work for the term, it was heartening to know he is capable of doing more.

Bullying once again became part of David's life. Year 8 and 9 boys have an amazing ability to find and torment the weakest of the species. David was often a target, and because of his reaction and inability to understand why people did what they did, he was always in trouble.

Wednesday 4 November 1998

David said some boys in Year 9 have been picking on him again and it is very noisy at school. He seems really happy at home, especially after we talked about what was going on and he didn't want me to get involved. I don't want him stressed, just to be happy at this stage. He has survived Year 8, probably not achievement-wise, but OK!

We continued on our mission to find natural therapies that would work for David. We were determined to find a solution based on his abilities to deal with his difference, not to prop him up with a synthetic, medical intervention.

This led me to the next naturopath who came highly recommended by a number of parents who I had become friends with at the school. The naturopath had a rather unorthodox method of determining what was going on for you, so with judgments aside, we made our first appointment. What she discovered was quite amazing.

Saturday 7 November 1998

David has a number of circulation problems, very low for a child his age. She felt the issues that arose after he was vaccinated may have been the cause. She prescribed some herbal remedy for those issues. Through muscle testing, she picked up immediately he was being teased at school. He also had a lot of fear around school, but there had been more tears about this last year (which was true).

Later I asked him if he was scared to go to school. He said, "Yes, all the time." I could have cried; no child should be scared of school.

There didn't appear to be an easy solution, and I was constantly on the lookout for answers.

I had to learn to listen to David, not through what he said but through what he didn't say. From there, I would rely on my intuition to see where I could take the conversation rather than being specific about the words he used. This meant taking time to be with him and continually searching my own feelings when he gave his usual one-word, monotone answers. Based on the answers he gave, I would then have to think very clearly about what questions to ask next so I could get a handle on what was really going on for him. Sometimes this could take hours or even days, when I would go over the conversation to try to get closer to an understanding. It was a matter of staying on top of what his emotion or stress was at any given point of time, and then trying to link it back to a thought or a feeling I had about a situation that had occurred.

So I started our bean-bag sessions again. Our morning and evening routines were exceptionally busy. We still only had one car. So each day began and ended with a very long car trip: first, dropping Gerry at work; then, driving David and Alissa to school; and, finally, Caitlin to day care. I would head back to our office to work or write; then every afternoon the routine would start all over again. Life was very busy and very tiring (for me!), and I had let our bean-bag routine slip during the process.

But I was starting to feel him move away from me, which is a normal response for boys at his age anyway; however, it was important I stayed connected to him. He was young boy going through puberty and that was OK, but I wanted to be able to understand this puberty versus Asperger's game. I felt that if I sat with him in his room, rather than just let him spend hours there all by himself, perhaps he would spontaneously start a conversation. He seemed quite comfortable with me just being in the room and would often chat to me about all sorts of things while playing on the computer or doing his homework. Some nights, the conversation would be talking about issues he was facing at school. Most nights they were just conversations about day to day things, homework or the book he was reading. Nothing really important, just connection conversations, and he seemed to enjoy our time together, without the girls being involved.

Monday, November 9, 1998

David seems to be doing well on the drops from the naturopath. We noticed a number of things this weekend.

He spent much less time on the computer and he actually got out and played touch football with the girls. He helped Gerry put up the swing set and figured out a way to sort out the problem when they discovered they had put the top bar on upside down!

Wednesday November 11, 1998

David seems to be getting more verbal. In fact, has been talking almost incessantly. Told me yesterday he figured he got 75 percent of his science test done easily even though he didn't study. Yesterday he got home before me and had not taken his key. When we got home, he just said, "Mum, I have been waiting for you for fifteen minutes. Where were you?" There was no stress in his voice, just questioning.

Monday, November 16, 1998

Yesterday we went to a friend's thirteenth birthday. It was a picnic. David seemed to enjoy himself and actually got a little more involved with the other kids. It was very pleasant sitting and chatting to some of the mums and hearing what really goes on in Year 8. Putting names to faces with a lot of the girls. The girls really seemed to include David, which was lovely. One of the mums said they were like little mothers around him…Ah, it was so nice to hear.

Tuesday, November 17, 1998

David came home very excited today. They begin auditions for the school musical on Saturday and Monday. He really wants a part in it. It is so wonderful to see him excited about something other than Nintendo. He just loves performing.

Wednesday November 18, 1998

David is certainly making many inroads. Last night he washed, dried, and put away the dishes, and before he went to school yesterday, he made his bed. He talked animatedly about auditioning for the musical. He was certainly a much happier child this week. He also announced he had received a B for Computers and Math…He was so proud of himself.

Friday, November 20, 1998

David's teachers are as surprised as we are at his good results. A 'B' each for Computers, Math, and English (could have knocked me over with a feather.) A 'C' for Science. Lord only knows what SOSE, Art, and Indonesian studies will bring, but I don't think he really cares. I am having trouble being enthusiastic or concerned about anything right now. Man I am tired.

Saturday, November 28, 1998

No wonder I was so tired. I have glandular fever, the naturopath says the only way I am putting one foot in front of the other right now is because I am fit. I am so tired, but at least I know what is wrong!

Wednesday, December 2, 1998

David came home very excited yesterday afternoon. He has a part in the musical! It is a chorus role, but he doesn't care; he is just thrilled to be in it, and we are thrilled to see him so excited. The musical takes place early in the new year, which will give him an incentive to go back to school!

SOCIAL SKILLS

In mid-1998, we found out about a new Social Skills program, and very quickly, Social Skills became David's life. He loved it. The Social Skills program ran with a group facilitator. Each week, a group of boys, all around the same age as David (and occasionally one or two girls) would meet and discuss feelings or any issues that had arisen during the week. The purpose of the Social Skills group was to teach the children how to interact in a normal social environment. They were taught how to start and participate in conversations, how to talk about their feelings, and often had time to debrief any incidents that had occurred during the week at home or at school.

The group would meet first and talk, and then would go out for an activity, which could be bowling, the movies, or miniature golf. Sometimes they would just go out for dinner and learn how to talk and exchange news with others.

He was at first, however, a difficult enrollee. The bullying and exclusion David was experiencing at school was now starting to really affect his personality, and he had begun to withdraw from life.

The coordinator of the program told me that many times during those first few months, David would sit at the outside of the group, totally disconnected. He responded many times in inappropriate ways, and at one point, she was going to request that he leave the group.

Her patience was amazing, however, and little by little, David started to interact. He is friends to this day with many of those young men who all began in the same Social Skills group.

Social Skills became a very sacred space, and whatever was discussed within the group stayed within the group. The boys experienced the normal interaction within a group of friends, where they also learned about emotions and how to deal with them, appropriate and inappropriate behaviors, and how to act just like neurotypical kids.

The boys (and the occasional girl) could say what they wanted to do in this space, and they knew it would go no further. As they began to trust the coordinator more, they opened up more, and many wonderful insights and friendships came out of the weekly Social Skills get-together.

Social Skills was a wonderful lifeline for David, and we will forever be eternally grateful to the team of wonderful carers.

Year 9—The Beginning of the End!

Well, we had managed to survive Year 8. Although the differences were now becoming extremely obvious, David was doing his best academically, considering the social and hormonal changes occurring in his life.

The holidays were always great "de-stressing" times for David, and because he was seldom asked over to a friend's place, I always ensured he participated in many organized activities. We enrolled David in a holiday drama program, which he really enjoyed, and he came home every night very animated and funny. I wished life could have been like that all the time for him.

In the last couple of days of the holidays, we also discovered a youth program at the local Police Citizens Youth Club. David had a great time going to the movies and the park and having a "pizza sleepover." He begged me to let him go on the final day as they were going to some rock pool, where they jumped from the rocks into the water. Apparently he was a little nervous at first, but eventually got the hang of it and jumped numerous times— it was a great self-esteem boost!

However, school resumed at the end of January, and all the fun of the holidays came to an abrupt end. Although David was very excited, because Caitlin was starting school, the excitement didn't last very long at all.

Monday, February 8, 1999 – Second week of Term One

David is not coping at all with Year 9. I looked at his business technology assignment last night, and it looks way beyond his capabilities.

Poor kid, he was really stressing last night—very teary. Only second week in and there are problems already. I am not sure how he will cope at all this year or whether any other school for that matter can cater for him. He says math, science, and drama are fine; SOSE and English are OK; but graphics and business technology are just way too hard.

Tuesday, February 9, 1999

David spent the day sleeping yesterday as he was very worried about school and couldn't sleep. He wants to change graphics for health and physical education, which I would rather he do anyway.

Friday, February 12, 1999

On Monday, we tried some aromatherapy essential oils for David. I burned them for him on Monday and Tuesday night. On Wednesday morning, he woke up and said, "I don't know what is in these oils, but they make me get to sleep and I wake up in the morning not at all tired!"

I wonder how long this therapy will work. As with everything we try, there is a reaction in the first week or so, but after a while, it wears off and David returns again to being stressed or tired.

Tuesday, March 2, 1999

David is traveling well physically right now and seems happy and content at home, sleeping well. He (we) completed his business technology assignment, and he (we) did his science assignment on Asperger's. It will be interesting to see his (our) marks!

Monday, March 8, 1999

It always seems like there is never a time to rest.

Yesterday started out nicely on the beach with friends. All the kids had a lovely time in the surf, and then we went back to their place for afternoon tea. The minute we were there, the boys started in on David.

He asked them if he could have a ride on their dirt bikes, and they wouldn't let him. Later they all went down to the creek for a swim. He came up about half an hour later very upset. The boys had been throwing rocks at him and then got on their bikes and were circling and terrorizing him.

I could hear the roar of the engines, but I didn't put two and two together until Alissa came running up from the creek screaming for us to come. I felt so bad that while we were having a glass of wine, he was being bullied and was terrified.

The same scenario occurs every time there is a bullying incident. The boys had their version and were adamant, which left David trying to explain, with his still limited vocabulary, what had happened. Alissa hadn't seen what happened as she was playing in the creek. The other parents, of course, chose the higher ground and made some comments about David reacting a little inappropriately. So we felt it was best to pack up and leave. As we were driving down the driveway, I saw the boys on their bikes, watching us leave, laughing and sniggering as we drove down the driveway.

David was very, very upset last night, and we promised him we would never go out there again. Why does this Asperger's have to affect our family so much? In everything, we do everything we want to do.

I feel for Alissa and Caitlin as well. We had to leave yesterday, when they were having a lovely time up until then. But they were upset and angry as well. It's not right that it should affect them. I held Alissa and Caitlin last night and let them know they were important too. Why is this so hard?

145

Monday, March 15, 1999

Last week was terrible week for David. After Sunday's episode, on Monday, he was picked on by a bunch of Year 10 boys at the musical. Tuesday he came home with his shirt ripped, Wednesday he and Nick had an altercation and Thursday he was in trouble for putting sharp objects on somebody's seat. Then at rehearsal, he was punched in the stomach for saying something to another boy.

We took him to the naturopath on Tuesday, and she gave him an affirmation to say, "I now bless everybody involved with my school." He doesn't think it is working...neither do I.

Saturday 20 March 1999

Parent–teacher interviews; both girls are doing very well and are in the top 10 percent of their classes.

David, on the other hand, is not coping at all. The only bright lights in his day are two teachers who really take time to try to understand him.

I had a chat to a mum today whose son, James, is similar to David. He is now at a technical college and doing well. I will investigate other avenues for David. Maybe a teacher aide will work for him. Who knows? How do you find the right school for a person who feels abandoned by those who should be supporting him?

I don't know what to do here. I need to do what is best for David. He needs the right people in his life to make it OK.

Saturday 10 April 1999

David has had a wonderful Easter holiday. He went to the Impact holiday program at the local Police Citizens Youth Club every day and just loved it. On Thursday as we were walking to the car, he said, "I just love coming here. They do such great activities."

On Thursday after they had been at the movies, they went to MacIntosh Island Park, and he was the only one to jump off the bridge. He said he wanted to prove to the others he was not afraid to do it. I think he may have wanted to prove that to himself.

Tuesday 18 May 1999

Yesterday we had our group meeting with some of David's teachers. It was very obvious at the meeting which subjects he is stressing about and which subjects he "'sort of" enjoys.

I believe much of his problem is he feels as if he is failing in so many areas, not just in academics but also in the whole friendship area, and it is all becoming too hard, so he is retreating into his own world. A couple of the teachers at the meeting didn't seem at all interested. But one or two had some good points to raise about David, his learning styles, and his sense of humor.

I know in my heart David can achieve success, because we have seen it when he is not stressed or feels confident. We need to keep seeking those opportunities.

During this time, I was still running seminars and trying to promote my books. The seminars meant that I was out of the house at night and not knowing how much money was coming into the house each week was causing a lot of stress. I was starting to feel like a failure because my business was going nowhere and I was constantly feeling as if I was being torn in two.

Wednesday, May 19, 1999—Another "Aha" moment!

Yesterday, the penny dropped while I was walking. David needs a mother to be there for him, to be his champion, and to believe in him. I spend too much time not feeling powerful or knowledgeable of this "difference." My job in this lifetime is to figure out what this means in our life. There is a message in all of this, I am not quite sure what yet, but I believe there is something profound here that goes just beyond Asperger's. There is something I am not seeing yet, but the frustration is so intense and the emotion is so intense, it has to mean something.

I can try to be successful by selling books and teaching seminars about all sorts of subjects, but what is the point if I have a child who is so unhappy?

I have been looking outside of myself to find answers when, in fact, I think the lessons and the answers are right here.

147

David's Asperger's syndrome is in our lives for a reason. I have absolutely no idea why, but I think if I keep asking the right questions, the answers will arrive. Is that it? Is that what this is, learning to ask the right questions and trust?

The parents from the Social Skills group David belonged to frequently met for picnics during the holidays. It was often a great afternoon of gossip and theories, of laughter and sadness. But we all understood each other and what we were going through. Even though our children were all different, we had a common experience that others just didn't understand. It felt good to be understood and not judged!

Thursday, June 24, 1999

It has been such a long time since I have had the time to write in this journal. So many things are happening we need to constantly re-evaluate where we are heading, and what we are doing.

Money is a huge issue all the time. David is going through a really tough time, both at school and with friends. It seems we are constantly trying to come up with one solution after the next. When that doesn't work, we try something else. But every now and then, something happens that makes me grateful for what we have. After the picnic today with the other AS boys and their families, I am so thankful we have David. He is so gentle, quiet, and deep thinking. The others' kids seemed so demanding, angry, and explosive individuals. They must be very hard to live with.

I decided in order to be more focused on David and his needs, I needed to put my seminar business on hold, and I began working for a home party plan company. I was then able to do many parties during the day and on weekends rather than being out at night; it made a difference to the house.

Wednesday, July 7, 1999

Things are moving for David. They have agreed to appoint a case manager for him to liaise with teachers. There has been such a difference in our family with me being home at nights. Caitlin is much happier, and David is more focused. He went to

148

school yesterday very nervous, but appeared to be a little more settled last night.

Tuesday, September 21, 1999

It is almost three months since I wrote in this journal and it has been an incredible three months.

Caitlin is growing up so much and is so cute and charming. Alissa's team won the Regional competition and then State Championships for Tournament of Minds.

David is changing so much, as tall as me now and quite solid, and is really starting to act like a teenager. When he doesn't want to do something, he just looks and stares at you, and it is really quite off-putting. There was great drama yesterday getting him to his Year 9 camp. He didn't want to go and was adamant that nothing we could say would make it any better. He finally got on the bus, without a word to us. I am praying he has a good time.

THE BULLYING CONTINUES

One day, toward the end of Year 9, I noticed bruises on David's arm, just above the elbow. "What happened here David?" I asked.

He said, "There is this boy in our class, and whenever I am standing in the line outside the classroom, he just continually punches me."

"*What!*" I said. "What does the teacher do?"

"Well," said David, "after the first time he did it, I hit him, and I got detention because he said I started it. So now when he punches me, I just try to ignore him."

"How long has this been happening?" was my shocked response.

"Oh," said David, "every lesson!"

Another trip to the school, another strategy, another sense of having to go to battle. I was glad it was the end of the year.

Wednesday, December 9, 1999

School is finally finished for 1999. I am going to change my whole perspective with David over the next eight weeks and focus entirely on making him calm, peaceful organized and ready for Year 10.

You could say I was the eternal optimist, after the holidays it didn't take long for reality to check in big time.

151

YEAR 10—CRISIS TIME

Year 8 was bad; Year 9, worse. Year 10 as a war looking for a place to explode.

The first few weeks of 2000 were incredibly stressful. David was dreadfully unhappy. I had thrown my hands up with trying to teach seminars and doing the home party plan business so I took a job as a telemarketer; Gerry took a sales job with a computer education company. Jobs we both hated but needed to do to keep a regular income coming in to the house.

It had been a terrible December and January. We had been trying desperately to still pay off all our bills from the boom years and subsequent recession, and we felt as though everything we touched turned to ash!

At Christmastime, we shopped at garage sales in order to have presents under the tree. The kids really wanted a trampoline, and we found one for fifty dollars. There were a few rusty springs and some bolts missing, which we were able to replace. We also managed to find lovely dresses and books to fill up the stockings. David was incredibly grateful for his computer magazines that came with free software. He didn't mind, and neither did the girls, they were amazing.

The year 2000 was the year of the "millennium bug." A propaganda campaign warned of devastation when all the computers in the world would click over at 11:59 on December 31, 1999, and would go to 0, wiping out all knowledge on hard drives. I remember being so disappointed at 12:01 on January 1, 2000,

153

when the electricity was still on—I had hoped the millennium bug might wipe out all records of our debts at the same time!

The stress was intense, made even worse by having to go to work each day in jobs we just hated, making us both feel not only failures in business but also failures as parents. None of the strategies seemed to work for David over an extended time. I guess in a way we were looking for a "cure," but there was none. We were looking for a quick fix and there were none of those either.

Once school started back at the end of January, our home life was incredibly unhappy. There were many arguments over money; many arguments over what was best for David; constant battles over homework and assignments; and many, many nights when I would question the reason why this was all happening to us. Life was a constant struggle, and we seemed to be stuck in a circle of stress.

I felt like I was doing high school all over again (and I had hated it the first time), sitting with David for hours every night, just trying to get through even the smallest amount of homework and assignments. Throughout this time, David began to withdraw more and more. It was harder and harder to reach him. I was tired all the time, and each week was a constant struggle to ensure we could just pay the bills and put food on the table.

David was spending less and less time with us. He would come home from school and go straight to his room. He would shut the door, close the curtains, and just lie on his bed. Trying to get him to take part in family activities was tough.

By this time, he was fourteen. Whenever we went somewhere now, he usually chose to stay at home. It was easier, for him and for us. Socializing with David became incredibly stressful. He preferred his own company, and if we went somewhere with friends and kids his own age, before long, there was an incident and we would have to pack up and go home.

I felt like we were losing him, and I was very concerned that we were going to end up with an angry, resentful teenager on our hands, like the Asperger's teenagers I had heard and read about. I was very fearful of what to do next, and I had no idea how to change it. Life was very stressful.

CRUNCH TIME

Have you ever noticed in your life, when there is a decision to be made or a change has to occur, the intensity to make that decision or make a change increases? Like all the energy in the universe moves into one direction, forcing a plan of action? This was just such a time.

Things were going from bad to worse. Gerry was tired, stressed, and very low. He hated his job and I hated mine. I was at my wits end, and David was teary and emotional all the time.

Three nights over two weeks changed my view of life and my beliefs about dealing with this "difference" forever. On the first night, Gerry was late getting home and I was incredibly stressed. David wouldn't even attempt to do his homework that night, and I knew he had an assignment due the next day. We had already been granted an extension twice on the assignment, and yet the process of getting the research done and the information on paper was just not happening. Caitlin was not well and was very clingy. Alissa was in her room, quiet, just doing her homework and trying her best to stay out of the bedlam.

I was running late for a meeting at the school. David and Caitlin ran to the door and both started screaming and crying, "Mum, don't go; stay with us."

I was yelling at Gerry for being late; he, of course, started to yell back at me saying that he was doing his best. With that, I drove out of the driveway and backed straight into the car parked across the road.

Message number one: crunch time!

One week later, it was my turn. Gerry and I were having a dreadful argument. It had been a rough week. Bills were piling up, and I couldn't imagine where we were going to find the money to fix our car, let alone the car I had damaged. I was so over living like this.

David was harder and harder to reach, and the stress to complete his assignments was peaking. He was withdrawing more and more into his room and refusing to even attempt any work, let alone communicate with us.

And on one particular night, I totally lost it.

Gerry and I were yelling at each other and Alissa walked out of her room and just started yelling, "Stop fighting; just stop fighting!"

I looked at her, grabbed the car keys, and drove off as Gerry was coming out of the front door, yelling at me to come back. I drove around for about half an hour and found myself at the lake, not far from our house. I drove the car onto the boat ramp and stopped. The tires of the car were touching the water.

I began to question what on earth life was all about. Why was this happening? Where were we going? Where was the picket fence? Was this what life was going to be like for the rest of my life?

The pain in my heart was unbearable. I could hardly breathe. I felt I couldn't do this anymore; I was tired, oh so tired and broken; my heart was broken. Everything felt painful. I couldn't see past the pain, and I couldn't pull myself out of the blackness.

My hand was resting on the parking brake of the car. For a moment, I allowed myself to imagine what it would be like to let the brake go. The car would just roll into the water; it was dark and very muddy water. The car would rest there for a few days and nobody would ever find it. It would be a quick death and it would end the pain.

I sat there for what seemed like an eternity, just looking at the water with my hand on the brake.

Suddenly in my mind, I saw Gerry without a wife, the children without their mother, and him trying to explain that it was my decision to leave. I saw my children's pain. I saw Gerry's pain. I started to cry. If I ended it, it would be easy for me, but I would be leaving my family in pain. My family meant the world to me. The love I felt from them at that time was extraordinary. My wonderful husband, my beautiful children—was this really what I wanted, to leave them because it was getting too hard?

I was going to figure this out somehow. I let the parking brake go, backed out of my parking spot and drove home.

I opened the front door; all the lights were out, except for the one in our bedroom. I walked in and Gerry was in bed already. He just looked at me, angry and relieved all at the same time. I sat on the bed, gave him a hug, and said, "I am so sorry, can we work this out together?" He looked at me with tears in his eyes and nodded.

Message number two: it's time for a change.

Two nights later, Gerry and I were lying in bed reading. David walked into our room and sat on the bed, and looking straight into my eyes and straight into my soul with his sad, big brown eyes, he said, "You know, Mum, sometimes I just don't understand the purpose of living!"

I sat straight up and hugged him.

Message number three: it was time for action.

The next morning, I kept him home and I made an appointment with the headmaster of the school. It was time to act, and the best thing I could think of doing was to bring David home and let him heal. Our family was on a collision course with disaster, and if we could remove at least one of the stressors, then perhaps we could all take time to breathe and to heal the pain.

So, we withdrew David from school.

That time was very difficult, and Gerry and I both did a great deal of soul searching. Many parents at the school questioned what we were doing. I would often walk up to my group of friends to find they would stop talking as I moved closer.

157

One of them actually challenged me. "Don't you think you are making this more difficult for David, rather than letting him sort this out? You are just making a rod for your own back, you know. What happens if he doesn't come back to school? There are very few jobs for people who don't finish Year 10!"

The soul searching was deep and intense, but it felt right; and the alternative, keeping him at school, I knew for certain, was not the right thing.

Again, I was totally running on my intuition. In my heart, I knew a time-out was what David needed, not to be pushed but be allowed to emerge. I just had to stay strong and trust that what we were doing was the right thing for him and for us.

I felt that we were losing him. We couldn't reach him anymore and I was concerned about his sense of self and his confidence. It was obvious any strategies we were trying to put into place wouldn't work if he had no sense of who he was.

David's whole life was about somebody yelling at him, somebody treating him badly. I just couldn't imagine how on earth anyone could maintain a strong sense of self if every day you are just terrified to go to school.

The bullying and exclusion were happening every day. David couldn't see a way out of it, and neither could I, but I knew keeping him there wasn't going to solve the issue. Each day that he spent at school, whatever sense of self we managed to pull together each night was lost within the first ten minutes of stepping inside the classroom.

I couldn't put my child through that pain anymore. It was too heartbreaking, and somehow I just knew being at school was not the right thing for him—the problem was, however, we didn't have another alternative.

So bringing him home was the first step, and if all else failed, home school was going to be the next alternative.

Home school, gosh, that was going to be a true test of my strength! But first things first. Let him get better and then we would tackle that issue!

A NEW PERSON EMERGES, A NEW FAMILY EVOLVES

Little by little, changes started to occur. During the first week, David pretty much stayed in his room all the time and slept. The times he did emerge, he would wander out the back and walk around in a big circle, usually with a large stick in his hand, just trailing along behind him. There was always a story going on in his head, but whenever I asked what he was talking about he would reply, *"Oh, nothing."*

The third week, he started joining us for meals again. He wasn't talking very much, but we insisted he at least sit facing the table and used the knife and fork properly. Other than that, we placed no demands on him at all.

By the fourth week, he started to ask Alissa and Caitlin questions about their day. Just small at first *"How was your day?"* He *was* not really concerned about whether they answered but was looking for ways to connect.

By the fifth week, he wanted to start coming shopping with me or join us to the park on picnics. He started wanting to sit with us and gradually began to engage in conversations again.

The staff at Social Skills started noticing a difference in David as well. Little by little, he started to get involved with the conversations; little by little, he seemed more aware of others and started interacting in small ways.

Gerry and I both started working on ourselves at the same time. My journal entries from that time talk of long conversations about our beliefs, about dealing with our anger and our sorrow. We spent a lot of time together and drew strength from each other as we made the conscious effort to deal with issues and blocks as they came up for us as we delved further and further into the understanding of who we were. During that time, I coined the phrase "like peeling layers of the onion." No sooner had we dealt with one big issue, then when another one would arise. At least we seemed to go through things at different times so only one of us was "stuck in our stuff" at a time!

After David had been home about eight weeks, we noticed massive improvements in our family's dynamics. We interacted with love and happiness. We started to tell jokes again, to dance again; our family was coming back from the brink.

We started to see David for who he was. He was thoughtful and responsive. His language began to improve, his sense of humor returned. His eyes started to sparkle again. He was interacting with us again, joking and playing with the girls. He had come back to us and he was whole. OK, now what?

A PLACE WHERE ANGELS LIVE

During this time, I started to teach a weight-loss motivation program at the local technical college which ran an adult education night school. I was beginning to feel I needed to get back to doing what I loved to do, for my own sanity and now because the drama in the house had stopped at night, I could effectively try and get my seminar career back up again.

While I was there one evening, I saw an information sheet about a Year 10 literacy and numeracy program for students who don't fit into the normal school program. The program allowed students to effectively complete Year 10, and then continue on at the technical college to learn a trade or enter a diploma course.

My interest was piqued. The next day, I made an appointment with the head of the program, and David and I went to inquire about the possibility of him participating.

David was fascinated by computers, and we believed naturally his strength lay in that area but first, he had to get his Year 10 certificate. So he began the program along with his best friend, who had also been diagnosed with Asperger's syndrome.

Even though David had made great progress at home with us, going back into a school environment still posed problems. David had trouble concentrating. He couldn't, stay focused on any topic that was outside his limited range of interests. It made all the sense in his mind, but others had trouble continually talking about the latest Mario Brothers game or the new TV show he loved, called *Big Brother*.

Even though he was only taking two subjects, time management and completing assignments were still huge issues.

David still had problems with comprehension when the teachers used large numbers of words to explain something. Even though there were only a small number of students in the classroom, he still had trouble staying focused. He often grasped the first one or two sentences of a topic, but if he didn't understand a word, or a word, was used in a different context to what he was used to, he just couldn't grasp the theory and would shut down altogether.

It took all of us a while to realize just because he looked at you and nodded, it did not necessarily mean that he understood what you were saying. Unless you actually asked him to relate back what he understood, very often all the words were lost and mixed up in his head.

He wouldn't ask questions because, for the most part, he didn't grasp what people were saying in the first place. The words all sounded OK, but once they were inside his head, they were all jumbled up and just didn't make sense.

Even though I knew that medication could perhaps help him concentrate, and sometimes I was tempted to try it all over again, I wanted him to come to terms with challenging himself and to stay focused without medication.

This time, because he was only at school for a few hours each day and then only for class, not for all the other things that fill up the school day, we wanted him to find his own way.

We wanted David to be whole, to become true to himself, and to come to terms with, and create strategies to deal with his emotions. If he was ever going to emerge from Asperger's syndrome, medication was not the answer. I knew it would only mask his ability to learn and experience emotions. It may take him longer, but we believed it was a better way to do it.

And besides, the teachers at the technical college were just angels. They tried all sorts of ways to get David to interact.

One day I had a call from one of the teachers, asking me to come in for a meeting. They were having problems getting David to engage in an assignment which was to create a survey and to analyze the results.

They had tried for weeks to get him to do something on this assignment but to no avail. Here we go again, I thought, but I was surprised to realize that this time it was different. We talked between us for a few minutes, so I could understand what they were trying to do, and we spoke about a few alternatives.

One of the teachers asked me what his interests were and I said, "Other than Mario Brothers, the only other thing he is passionate about at the present time is that dreadful TV show *Big Brother*."

With that she sat straight up. "That's perfect. All the kids here love *Big Brother*. We will ask David to create a survey about *Big Brother* and what people think about it."

I couldn't believe the difference between the two systems, the school and the tech college. To his teachers at the tech college, it wasn't about the curriculum; it was about assisting these young people to engage in learning. How they reached the outcome wasn't important. The process, which was based on the premise of "competent" or "not yet competent," was a wonderful alternative for an Asperger's child; it was such an amazing change.

David, by the way, loved the assignment. He came home that afternoon, sat straight down at the computer, and didn't move for hours. He came up with a list of questions, how to run the survey, and how to group all the results. He loved it and was so proud of his "competent" result.

Life was better, but not all was plain sailing.

The program was not just for kids like David, but was also for kids who, for many reasons, found school not to their liking, either because of learning differences or behavioral issues. Hence, David, not fully recognizing the dangers of being "in somebody's face," would often find himself surrounded by boys who really did know how to look after themselves.

One day, I picked David and his friend up from tech and I overheard the conversation coming from the backseat.

"Dave, sometimes you can't win fights by yourself."

David replied, "I was ready to take him on. It's just he got a lucky punch."

I waited till we got home before I said, "What do you mean 'lucky punch,' David?"

After a big breath and sigh, he told me that he had walked past a large group of boys who were all smoking. David had a particular disgust of smoking. He hated the smell, and the constant health warnings convinced him anybody who smoked was an idiot (a strong belief he still has today). However, back then he had no understanding of tact. So if somebody was smoking, he just told that person what he thought!

On this particular day, when David and his friend walked past this very large group of very large boys, David happened to mention rather loudly that he thought smoking was stupid and that if anybody smoked, that person was an idiot.

Apparently, within seconds, both boys were circled by this group, and one boy in particular decided that he was going to "deck" David.

David immediately began to think he was his Power Ranger hero and went straight into fight stance and with the challenge laid before him; the boy reacted—landing a huge punch right in the middle of David's stomach. Teachers who were parading in the grounds stepped in to ensure nothing more serious occurred.

"You what, David?" was my hysterical response. "For goodness sake, David, these boys are twice your size. What would have happened if they all had taken you on? What on earth were you thinking? David, this is serious." I did notice somewhat during the tirade that my heart was beating fast and the pitch of my voice became a little higher.

He sat very still and didn't say anything. Finally I said "David, why didn't you tell me about this before?"

"Because I knew you would respond just like you are now," was his deadpan response.

MY BOY IS CHANGING

The Year 10 Literacy and Numeracy certificate was for a semester only, but David needed a little longer, so he took the rest of the year to complete the course. He was getting the hang of this learning thing and was starting to really enjoy the process of achievement, and so in 2001, we enrolled him in Certificate One, Information Technology; there was a light at the end of the tunnel.

We met with the disability services coordinator, and she was the intermediary with the lecturers, keeping an eye on David and assisting the tutors in comprehending that sometimes David could not understand questions or tasks. The model was also different as this time he had to negotiate lecture theatres rather than classrooms.

He was still behind with his organizational skills and found achieving deadlines on the more complicated assignments very challenging. However the model used was based on competency. It was not a matter of achieving A, B, C, or fail; it was simply a matter of repeating a task until you had achieved mastery. It was perfect!

After a long, challenging learning experience, in February 2002 David enrolled in the Diploma of Multimedia, and it was a great course for him. He just loved digital video and sound editing, which requires sitting at a computer for hours on end, watching less than ten seconds or so of film and sound at a time, and making the required changes. It was perfect for him. He also loved making movies and for his final assignment, he wrote, directed, and starred in, along with his best friend, a very funny spoof of alien movies. Although very quirky, it was also very entertaining.

He didn't win any major awards at the end of the year with it, but we were very proud of him and had two "Oscar" statues made—one for him, Best Director, and one for his friend, Best Actor—and presented the trophies to the boys at a dinner we hosted at our home, where we showed the movie to family and friends.

GRADUATION

It was a letter I could never have imagined ever arriving. I had just completed my morning walk and had collected the mail.

At the time, we lived in a house set back from the road and overlooking a lake, so the trip to the mail box was actually a bit of hike. When I got down to the deck, I stopped to actually look at the envelopes in my hand: phone bill, power bill, newsletter from some organization that I had joined ages ago and couldn't quite remember why they were still sending me information I never read anyway, and then there was the letter addressed to Gerry and I, an official looking letter from David's college.

Oh dear, I thought, was this something I really wanted to open? I had been so used to receiving letters in the past calling for a meeting with us about David or telling us that he was late in returning something; that this letter could be something different just never occurred to me.

It is with great pleasure we invite you to the graduation of your son David ... mortar board and gowns are available for hire...

The memories of all those years of pain and heartache flooded back. The questioning, the arguments, the stress, the tears, and here it was packaged up in a letter explaining what time David had to be at the ceremony, the costs, the require-ments, and that he would be wearing an academic gown and mortar board!

167

I am not sure if other parents go through the same feelings when their child is graduating. Do they also go through the same sense of relief, joy, disbelief, and "eureka" moment I was feeling? Do they also cry tears of joy and remember their child's moment of birth, first step, first word, first day of school, and first day of high school?

Do they remember when it felt there were no options available? When life was tumultuous and sad? When they used to lie in bed at night and wonder if it was worth getting up the next day? When they questioned who they were and whether they were good enough to be a parent?

Perhaps they do, but for me, on that warm Saturday morning with the lorikeets singing and the gum trees swaying in the wind, it was a moment I will remember for the rest of my life.

We had made it. We had made it in one piece. We had made it as a whole family. We had made it as a complete family. How incredibly proud I felt at that moment.

ONWARD AND UPWARD

After graduation, we took the next step and David enrolled in the Bachelor of Multi-Media degree at university, doing only three subjects a semester.

Again, with Disability Services assistance, David became quite adept at getting himself around the university and learning all about deadlines for assignments, one night even pulling an 'all nighter' at the university with members of his group, to complete an assignment on time.

During this time also, another world opened up for him: soccer.

David was not at all into sport. In fact, after the soccer incident when he was a child, the whole idea of team sports was just like a nightmare in his eyes. However, as part of the Social Skills program, a number of the boys played in a soccer team. The coach issued a challenge for David, to try soccer for six months and if he didn't like it after that, then he could pull out.

Every week, I drove David to soccer practice at the various venues. At first he complained about going for training but after six months he was converted.

His coach was fantastic. He expected the boys to train and act just as any soccer team composed of neurotypical children. They were expected to be on time, to train hard, to be polite, to listen to their coach, and to treat each other with respect.

The boys loved it and did whatever he told them to do. If they didn't train hard enough, he made them do push-ups. If they did something inappropriate, he made them run laps of the oval. It was great training for all the boys, and the one thing their coach insisted on was that they learned about being part of a team, one thing children with Asperger's often miss out on.

Through soccer, David became very fit, attending many Special Olympics Soccer carnivals throughout Queensland.

In 2005, David attended trials to choose the Queensland team, to play in the National Special Olympic Games to be held at the end of 2006 on the Gold Coast. The training was very intense; there were only fifteen spots available, for boys from all over the southeastern Queensland district trialing.

At the final day of selections, David was really focused. He had been training for weeks. He and a friend had been getting together on the days where there was no training to get in a little extra practice, and he felt very ready for the trials.

But in the first ten minutes of the first game, disaster struck. David went to kick the ball and slipped, twisting his ankle. He was devastated. All those weeks of training down the drain.

His coach and his friends on the team did their best to console him, but he felt he had blown his chances. He was sad but, at the same time, was quite mature about the whole incident. "Oh, well," he said. "Perhaps I have created a spot for somebody else who might have missed out." What a great attitude!

Toward the end of January 2006, David received a letter. He walked into the living room, sat on the couch, read three lines, and literally jumped over the back of the couch with excitement.

"I made it. I've made the team. I will be representing Queensland!" It was so exciting. What a great achievement, twisted ankle and all!

Then began weeks of very intense training and fund-raising.

Much of the fund-raising consisted of "coin drops." Members of the team took turns to stand in the local shopping centers, asking people for donations of coins to assist them in offsetting the costs of competing. David was very hesitant at first, and the coordinator of the fund-raising had to use all her persuasive skills to get him to participate while he used every avoidance skill possible to get out of it.

However, once he started, there was no stopping him, and in one day, he raised more money than anybody else. Once he got the hang of it, he felt quite comfortable in asking people for donations—he became a fund-raising champion.

The Special Olympics National Games was a huge event with competitors from all over Australia. The Queensland soccer team, in particular, was very impressive. The coach insisted on discipline and that they looked and acted just like a professional soccer team—and they did, taking out the gold medal.

Watching the boys standing on the winners' podium and receiving their gold medals was simply a goose-bump moment. Cheering, waving, and crying, each of the boy's families stood proudly and sang the national anthem... this was the crowning moment, an incredibly proud event for all.

Many of the boys from the team were then selected to represent Australia at the International Special Olympics held in Beijing in 2007. David turned down the opportunity to play as he wanted to concentrate on his university studies and didn't want to defer the semester in order to travel. We were disappointed, and we would have loved him to experience the travel, but his mind was made up. He felt that if he deferred, it would take him too long to get back into the flow again, and although we were disappointed he wouldn't be going, we were also very proud of the mature decision and the way he made the decision.

It was a choice. He knew it was a choice, and he made the choice he felt was better for him, after weighing all the possibilities.

He had come a long way and we were very proud of whom he had become, but it was at his twenty-first birthday party where we truly saw what an amazing young man he is.

171

After we and his friends had made speeches about him, David stood up and thanked every person individually in the room with a little story about how they have been there for him and how grateful he was they had been in his life.

And at the end of his speech, he turned to Gerry and I and said, "But most of all, I want to thank my parents, because they believed in me, fought for me, supported me throughout my life. Without them, I would not be standing here in front of you tonight. Mum and Dad, thank you!"

GIRLS AND RELATIONSHIPS

The next great hurdle for David was in navigating the complicated world of girls and relationships. During his second year of university, he met a girl and they started dating.

A few months into the relationship, he asked us if he should tell her he had Asperger's. We talked about it for a while. I was concerned it may affect her or her parent's view of him and I didn't want him to be hurt.

When I asked him what he wanted to do, he said, "Mum, I really like this girl, but I can't have an authentic relationship with her unless I am honest. Asperger's is a part of who I am. I can't hide that from her because it would mean she only knows a part of me, not the whole of me!"

He just simply amazed us with his insight, caring and incredible understanding of who he was. He learned a lot about relationships during that time. However, this relationship was not to be and we were exceptionally proud of him when he was trying to come to terms with breaking up with this girl. He was so intent on finishing the relationship without hurting her and, at the same time, finding his sense of truth and integrity. She made it tough for him however; calling many times at night and generally making life very difficult. However, he never wavered and continued to treat her with kindness and compassion until eventually we had to step in and call her parents to ask them to intervene.

But we were so proud of how he handled it. All those years of not knowing whether or not we were doing the right thing when we chose not to use medication ended right there. We had done the right thing; we had allowed him to discover his own emotions, learn about and understand others people's pain and in doing become compassionate and thoughtful of others.

We had raised a simply outstanding young man.

MY SPECIAL MOMENT

We have a tradition in our family that Gerry and I started when we were first together. When you give somebody a card, you also write a special thought, meaning, or insight about that person.

At my fiftieth birthday party, Gerry gave me a poem that he had framed. The children also presented their special cards written with such beautiful emotion and sentiment.

David's card, however, was simply amazing. This card was written by a boy who didn't speak until he was four, was from a boy who supposedly didn't understand emotion, or other people's feelings, and was from a boy who had experienced so much hurt and exclusion in his life. This is what my son wrote:

Dear Mum…

There is so much stuff I need to thank you for over these years, and I don't think this card is big enough to express what I have to say.

You have always looked out for me in even the most difficult stages of my life. I think to me you were even more than just my Mother, you are like my Guardian Angel, always being there when I needed you the most.

I know of many children at school who turn to you for help and support and it really makes me proud and fortunate to think you are truly a 'super mother'.

I'm pretty sure your life story over the last 50 years you've had your fair share of hits and misses but you know through your life experience how to help me and everyone else in our family.

You are a true inspiration.

I love you, Mum

David.

OK, right, yes, I cried!

2010

A t the end of 2007, David decided he wanted to focus more on film making and digital video editing and decided to change his degree. In December 2010 he graduated from university with a Bachelor of Screen and Film Production Degree. He is an avid contributor to the Web site YouTube and has many followers on numerous social media sites.

He has traveled interstate many times by himself; including organizing a trip to Perth to work at a technology expo as part of his work experience, and organizing and attending many You Tube gatherings. He had worked part-time at the Movie World theme park on the Gold Coast during the holidays and enjoyed the experience immensely.

There is no doubt David still has Asperger's, although most people tend to think he is just quiet, shy, or introspective. He still exhibits some Asperger's tendencies. However, he is very resourceful and lets nothing stand in his way to achieving what he wants. There are still some downsides to his difference. He gets stressed if we have not been clear in our communication or when he feels we have not understood exactly what he wants. However, if he is feeling overwhelmed, he will go outside for a walk and allow his stress to dissipate.

He still finds creating friendships face-to-face a challenge, although he has made very good friends online and often communicates with people all over the world regularly via Twitter,

YouTube, or Face book. He also has a couple of close friends who sometimes spend the weekends together. He finds social interaction at noisy venues, such as night clubs or hotels, difficult, although he has developed good coping skills that make him look like he is focused and attentive.

David is not comfortable with small talk or social chitchat; however, he will talk for hours on subjects that interest him.

He has maintained his great interest in politics and world events and is very confident in expressing his views. And he shows wonderful compassion and understanding towards others.

He is very creative and expressive when telling a story or when creating a video for an assignment for university or a YouTube clip, a throwback perhaps to those times when he would wander around the tree talking to himself creating stories in his mind. During those times, he was not in the least bit concerned about what others thought or in any way concerned by what was going on around him at the time. Today, he creates the most amazing, off-the-wall stories, perfect for much of the subject matter he had to develop for his degree.

David still has Asperger's but he has developed socially acceptable coping strategies, which allow him to interact in group situations or in work environments. However, he is quite comfortable going to movies, various events or travelling on his own. He is very comfortable with his own company, a skill many of us neurotypicals still have trouble coming to terms with.

Recently I asked David what he could remember about his early years with Asperger's, and in particular, I asked him if he remembered what it was like to be on medication.

"I don't remember the actual days or weeks," he said. "But what I do remember is I didn't like taking those tablets. It made me feel different from who I was. It gave me headaches and I couldn't sleep at night. I liked myself better when I wasn't taking medication."

DAVID'S GIFT TO US AS PARENTS

When Gerry and I were first married, I don't believe I had any strong or outstanding views about what being a parent really was. I had read all the birthing books (and that really didn't get me anywhere!), but for the rest of the parenting business, I think I pretty much relied on using the common, shared values passed down from my parents.

When David came along, Gerry and I had to constantly reevaluate our parenting because the actual role we were supposed to assume was not really clear. I watched other people with their children and it looked so easy. They didn't have to teach their child how to socialize. They didn't have to explain over and over what things meant. Their children communicated with them easily and didn't overreact to noise or overstimulation. It felt as if we were always on guard, watching and waiting for the time when we would have to jump in and solve an issue, or talk to a teacher, or leave a social gathering, or save him from a bully. We needed to be constantly on guard, constantly vigilant.

After the Year 10 crisis, we finally grew to realize that in order for us to be the best possible parents we could be; we first needed to be the most self-actualized and self-aware individuals we could be. There was a real risk that we could both get lost in the drama and the emotion that surrounded us at the time. We needed to find the common ground where we, as two people in an authentic relationship, could support each other to find our own truth and our own sense of self, not only as individuals but also as parents and as a couple.

We needed to teach David to understand emotion, so for that to happen, we need to be absolutely 100 percent clear on our own emotions. We needed to understand why and how our emotions and beliefs affected our reactions to certain situations and stimuli. There was no room any longer in our relationship for façade or game playing. We had to get issues out on the table so when we were faced with a challenging situation or decision we were both on the same page and working together. We had to find out who we were first, then bring that knowledge to our relationship, so we could be the parents David needed us to be. We had to stand up as individuals so that we could stand up as a couple.

When we finally decided we needed to work together on this, we spent many nights talking, reading and learning about beliefs and emotions and where and how they manifest in our lives. It was during this time, I realized that I had blamed myself for David having Asperger's syndrome. For many years, I felt it was something I had done, hadn't done, could have done, or should have seen. I spent so long trying to fix this issue, spinning on an axis, running from one solution to the next that I was wearing myself out. But because I blamed myself, I turned that blame outwards, pushing it on to others; I wanted to blame Gerry and make it his fault, or the medical profession's fault, or somebody's—anybody's — fault. The blame then manifested as anger because I felt I was powerless to fix it. I realized then that the cause of so many arguments that Gerry and I had, was about those feelings of powerlessness and blame.

The turning point for me was the "aha" moment while on that morning walk when I suddenly realized that I had spent way too much time seeking answers from others rather than feeling confident enough to trust myself. I was continually looking in the past, trying to find the reason why this was in our lives, rather than accepting it and focusing on creating solutions for issues as they arose.

Blame is such a debilitating emotion, whether it is blaming yourself or others. The fact is this: sometimes things happen that just suck! So you have two options: create a solution or don't. But moaning about it and looking for a person to blame is not only a waste of time, it stops you from feeling empowered.

Our role, as parents, was to give David all the authentic, powerful inner tools to allow him to navigate his own life. We were the only people who could do that. Those tools were not going to magically appear from somewhere else and they were not going to miraculously appear overnight. This was a long term commitment. We accepted this challenge the moment this child was born. Once we made the decision to be parents, then we made that decision for life.

David could best learn about love, commitment, compassion, and forgiveness if he could see these in our relationship and could understand what they meant because he was surrounded by them. In order to be the parents we needed to be, it was crucial we were clear on our own path of self-awareness. In order to teach him those skills, they needed to be so real in our lives.

Our job was to become the people we wanted David to be.

An authentic life is not measured by the things we have; it measured by the relationship we have with ourselves and with others. Each and every emotion you have starts from a thought, a belief, or an experience. When David reacted explosively or inappropriately, there was always a reason. Our role as his parents was to get beyond the reaction and figure out why. In so many cases, the reason he responded the way he did had absolutely nothing to do with the incident at hand. Something else was usually at the bottom of it.

So the same holds true for us as well. Behind every action we take is a response to a belief we have about ourselves or about others. That reaction is driven by an emotion, and in order to understand the emotion, we need to get to the belief or thought behind it and deal with it. Every challenge that arises in your life becomes an opportunity to create more knowledge about you and about those around you.

Why? Because, in the end, what happens to you is not important, but how you handle it is.

Gerry and I had two choices. Either we were going to work this relationship out or we were not. It was simple. There were so many times during those years when one of us wanted to walk out the door with a suitcase packed when it became too hard, when the arguments became over whelming and we both wondered if we truly did like each other anymore.

But we also came to the realization that whatever we didn't come to terms with in this relationship; we would simply carry on to another. Running away wasn't going to solve the issue - we needed to work on ourselves and find our own truths before we could make any sustainable change to our relationship. We made our choice to do it together. We understood the only way we could teach David about love, was by being loving. The only way we could teach David how to be compassionate was for us to demonstrate compassion, and the best way to teach David about forgiveness, by being forgiving.

So we got to work and found ways in which we could come to grips with our own issues. It was important we dealt with our own beliefs and emotions, and we chose to find our own ways of dealing with them.

Gerry became very involved with a self-empowerment group for men and spent time discovering the complexities of masculinity in this generation. He attended many seminars designed to help men deal with anger, sadness, and emotion. It was through this experience that he was able to come to terms with many issues of his childhood and subsequent years of his life.

For me, writing was very cathartic, and the process of daily or weekly journaling was, as I realize now, essential in allowing me to come to terms with certain beliefs and patterns that dominated my life. I spent time exploring my passion for teaching and writing, taking part in many self development and presentation skills seminars as well as studying for a Diploma of Professional Counseling and speaking to others about Asperger's syndrome.

In order for any relationship to work, it is essential that two self-actualized, self-aware individuals come together prepared to support each other. This is especially the case when a couple is faced with a challenge such as Asperger's syndrome, and sadly many marriages in this situation do not survive. The tragedy is that the one thing that children with Asperger's need to see, more than anything, is how love works, and what better way to learn that lesson than modeling their parent's relationship.

Any challenge in your life has a gift attached to it and the way you find that gift is to ask yourself the right questions. What is it I really want? What do I need to do to create the right solution? Is there something going on here that I need to look at? Is there an underlying belief that causes me to react this way? Each and every challenge has a gift; what you do with it is your choice.

THE STEPS ALONG THE WAY

A s with any change in your life, there are a number of steps and processes that make it all work. Having a child of difference is hard work, emotionally and physically. In order to cope, you, as the parent, must put your health and your well-being first, so you have the energy to be whole and present. Toward the end of my fitness instruction days, I began to realize that fitness, health, and weight were more than just the food you put in your mouth or the exercise you did but, rather, was about the whole person. In order to be truly energetic, happy, and whole, there are four aspects to authentic fitness —physical, emotional, spiritual, and intuitive. Each of those aspects are as important as the other and need to work together to ensure that you are strong enough to deal with issues as they arise.

THE FOUR STEPS TO AUTHENTIC FITNESS

1. Physical Fitness

Our bodies express our emotions and our beliefs. When a negative emotion is trapped in the body, it manifests as pain, illness, or tiredness. While being fit is certainly not the panacea to all ills, being physically fit gives you energy and helps create endorphins or the positive thoughts to help you deal with the emotions and stressful situations in your life.

During the early days of David's diagnosis, I used my early morning exercise sessions to clear my head and my heart of pain and to create a space where the ideas could flow, where the optimism could return, and where I could create enough energy to face the day. I exercised with a group of mothers, each going through the ups and downs of motherhood, parenting, and relationships, so our exercise time not only became our fitness time, but also time for a great chat and for solving each other's problems. It was a perfect union!

To this day, physical fitness is an essential aspect of my weekly routine. If something is bothering me or I can't think of a solution to something going on in our lives, the first thing I do is head off for a walk or spend half an hour working out with weights. I start with the belief that I will have a solution to the issue by the time I finish, and I usually do.

Physical exercise helps you feel strong and centered, gives you energy, and allows you to release stress from your body. Being confident, optimistic, insightful, and resilient require just as much physical strength as it does emotional strength.

Everybody needs physical fitness in his or her life for energy and health, but parents of children with Asperger's need to be physically fit so that they have the energy to cope with the extra demands. Physical fitness must be a priority. It saves you energy and time in the long run!

2. Emotional Fitness

The next step is emotional fitness: discovering what causes a negative emotion to surface and then creating a strategy to deal with the belief behind it.

In the early days, our whole household felt as though it was filled constantly with negative emotion. I remember once apologizing to David after one particularly emotion charged evening. I felt as if I was always yelling at him, especially when the sadness or tiredness became overwhelming. I sat on the end of his bed and said, "David, I am so sorry I yell at you all the time." He looked at me with his enormous brown eyes. A quizzical look came over his face. He said, "When do you yell at me?" I almost fell off the bed!

Each negative emotion has a gift in its intensity. The challenge is to find out what it is. Because I blamed myself, the anger I felt manifested because I couldn't make life better. I couldn't stop or fix this; I couldn't make the world treat David differently.

As a parent, I felt it was my job to make my children happy, to create a world where they felt special, unique, safe, and happy. To watch my son go through pain, confusion, and exclusion made me feel inadequate and helpless, which manifested as anger. My anger was my frustration at my perceived inability to make things right. At the bottom of that emotion lay blame, because I believed that I had caused the problem in the first place.

Emotions are formed from beliefs we have about ourselves. Recently, I was asked by a businesswomen's group to develop a seminar series on the skills of public speaking. As with all things in life, I look first to the emotions surrounding any issue. In public speaking, the first emotion most people have to overcome is fear. Public speaking sits very high on people's most feared experience, behind heights, spiders, and death!

In the seminars, I use a tool called "reframing," and with that topic, I use a flip chart signifying an iceberg. The top third of the iceberg represents emotions; the bottom two-thirds are the beliefs that drive the emotions. The emotion that drives us at any given point is simply linked to a belief sitting just below the surface. When you reframe the belief or look at it in a different way, the emotion changes. In the case of public speaking, until you get to the core belief that drives the fear, you can forget about trying to teach any skills.

The same analogy holds true in all aspects of life.

The negative emotions dominant in my life in those early days were blame, anger, and sadness. I wanted to turn the blame I felt outward; I wanted to rage at the world; I wanted the world to change; I wanted people to change. I was angry at the world, and I was angry with me. I was sad this life was not how I intended. I was sad that I couldn't make it any better for David. I was sad, angry, and in pain, because I felt helpless.

I believed that Asperger's in our lives was going to be hard and that the world would never change to accept my son and the way he viewed the world. Through writing and asking questions, I realized underneath those beliefs was another whole set of beliefs about life never going the way I wanted: that life was hard, that I had no right to happiness or success. It was like peeling an onion really; it just seemed as if I would get to one belief and find another one sitting right underneath it. I could drive myself nuts trying to figure it out or just decide to change the belief.

So I did, and when I changed my belief about Asperger's, incredibly the world changed. (Funny, that!).

I made the decision to stop thinking about this as a disability and a problem and instead started looking at it as a difference—a gift. I decided to start a new habit; a new way of dealing with life called Living in the Question. Whenever an issue or problem arose, instead of falling into the negativity of it, I got into the habit of asking myself the questions, "What is it I need to see here?" and "What is it I need to understand?"

As I became more conscious of asking questions, rather than falling into despair or hopelessness, the more the answers appeared. As more answers appeared I began to realize Asperger's had given us the tools to deal with any challenge which came our way.

I couldn't fix this difference. It was not my issue to fix in the first place; rather, my responsibility was to help David navigate his life the best way he could. I wasn't to blame; I did the best job I could do at the time, with the knowledge I had at the time. With each situation that arose, I gained more knowledge. When I had more knowledge, I did things differently.

When I started to look at the world through different eyes, my world began to change. Each time an emotion arose, I set about to get to the core belief surrounding the emotion. Slowly, my beliefs about myself started to change, along with the way I spoke and the way I thought. Every time a self-blaming thought or the feeling of hopelessness or helplessness arose, I changed the pattern and the words, using simple, powerful statements such as; I create my own reality; I have power over how I deal with this issue; and, my favorite, I always find a solution, always.

When a negative emotion arose, I would ask myself the question, "What am I really angry/sad/frustrated about?" Over the years, Gerry and I both became very confident about doing this with each other (although, I might add, it took a little practice and a lot of patience to figure out just exactly how and when to ask the question—we are still human!). However, once I understood what was causing the anger, the blame, the sadness, or the pain, and I mean truly got to the bottom of the issue and could understand it, then things changed quickly.

The solution to any situation is always in front of you, but it is often masked by a random emotion throwing the veil over your eyes so you can't see the solution.

David still had Asperger's, that didn't change, but how we viewed it changed. Once we changed how we viewed the challenge we had been given, we began to manifest all the opportunities available and all the people who could help us.

Emotional fitness allows you to find your own solutions to any challenge that arises. It happens on such a regular basis in our lives now that we just take it for granted. But I know this to be true: you always have the answers to any challenge that arises in your life; you just have to trust in your innate abilities to find the answers.

3. Spiritual Fitness

The third part of the equation is spiritual fitness. That place where you are able to connect with something within you that is whole, peaceful, quiet, and free. It is the place where resilience is created and optimism reigns. It's that place where unconditional love just flows and forgiveness comes easily and naturally—the ability to forgive yourself, forgive the world, forgive the situation, forgive the emotion, and forgive whatever is going on in your life.

The power of forgiveness is so life-changing, and on one particular day, the power of forgiveness changed the relationship David and I had forever.

When David was twelve, just before he left primary school, I used to get very sad for him during school holidays as he was often left alone. Although he received the odd invitation to go to somebody's house, the invitations were few and far between. Those friends he did have were from families who were far wealthier than we were, and they would often go away on their holidays. So David often spent the holidays on his own. This was made even more difficult because Alissa often spent her holidays on sleepovers and with friends.

So on one particular school holiday, I was desperate to find an activity David liked, so I booked him into a computer day camp. It was, at the time, very expensive and took all our available cash to register him for the weeklong course.

One morning we were running late for both his class and my class at the gym. I needed to get to the gym to teach a 9:30 class and David was wandering around in his usual daze. I rushed out to the car and strapped Caitlin in her car seat. This was always a struggle because she hated it and getting her into the seat with the seatbelt done up took superhuman effort! I then ran back inside and yelled at David to hurry up. We were already late and should have left ten minutes before.

We lived in a split-level house at the time, with about four steps separating the living room from the bedrooms. I ran back into the house, yelling at him to hurry up. I was already stressing about how much this computer course was costing, Caitlin was in the car screaming, and I just hate being late. I again yelled at him to hurry up and as I got to the stairs, he met me. He was standing there just looking at me; it was one of David's not-with-it days.

"What are you doing?" I yelled (think fishwife). He just looked at me and said, "What?"

I remember being so angry. All at once, all the frustration and anger erupted and I pushed him down the stairs. He fell backward, just managing to keep his footing. He just stood there and looked at me. I couldn't believe what I had done.

When we finally got in the car, I was so overwhelmed with guilt and shame that I couldn't say anything. I just drove out of the garage and kept my eyes firmly on the road ahead. After about five minutes, I looked over at David and saw a single tear running down his cheek. He just looked at me with huge big brown eyes and said, "Mum, I am so sorry I make you so angry."

The pain in my heart was agonizing. I pulled the car over, hugged him, and cried. "David, I am just so sorry. It's not you. It's a lot of other things. I should never have pushed you. That was wrong of me. I am so sorry." I truly meant it; my heart just ached.

At that point, I truly understood how people snap, how sometimes things happen in families that are, on the surface, unforgivable. I also understood I had been to a place where I could truly harm my children. It was in that instant dark, intense emotional moment, where I needed to forgive myself for the darkness that dwelled inside.

Spiritual fitness is the part of life that helps us to recognize and acknowledge both ends of the spectrum. I couldn't be whole, yet deny at the same time that there was a part of me that was, for want of a better word "dark." But I could also forgive myself for having those dark moments. I could also forgive myself for being angry with the world. I could also forgive the fact that this had been given to us and that sometimes I didn't want it any more. I could also forgive myself for the times I didn't cope very well, for the times when I wanted to be angry, and for the times I felt helpless.

I can balance this dark and light in my life and know that I sit in the middle and that only I choose my next step. I know that some things bring up the dark and some things bring up the light, and I realize always that I have a choice.

Spirituality, whatever that means in your life, grounds and connects you and gives you a purpose and a place of calm, either through meditation, movement, prayer, or whatever means you use. It's the quiet space within that allows you to see the wonderful: the sunset, the beauty of the landscape, the joy in a child's' eyes, the symphony of the laughter when the whole family finds something hilarious in a funny moment.

It's allowing yourself to breathe, to sense a connection to whatever source holds true for you. Spiritual fitness creates resilience and optimism and is about being whole and accepting of who you are. It's OK to feel angry, it's OK to feel sad, and it's OK to scream at the world because life is so unfair. But spiritual fitness connects you to your inner knowledge and peace, helping you find the space that opens your heart and allows you to deal with issues that arise for you so much easier. Resilience is that all-knowing place; that place in your heart where you know that no matter what happens, you have the optimism within you to overcome even the most challenging issues.

4. Intuitive Fitness

The fourth aspect of whole fitness is intuition, your inner solution to navigating any situation.

I traveled overseas when I was younger. On those travels, I remember so many times when my intuition guided me and steered me clear of some potential problematic situations. Often I didn't know there was a problem until later. But somehow I always managed to find the right thing to do.

It is a skill we have encouraged with all our children. That feeling, sense, or thought that arises when something doesn't feel right or you need a solution to a challenge that has arisen.

It's like tuning in your radio to the correct frequency and recognizing when it's not tuned in properly.

However, as with any aspect of fitness, intuition is a practiced art. It requires you to be physically, emotionally, and spiritually fit and strong; so that you are able to sense when the right solution or opportunity appears for you, and then have the confidence to trust it.

When we needed something or somebody to show up in our lives, we learned to ask the question as clearly and specifically as we could. The solution often wasn't what or how we imagined it to be, but without exception the right person or solution for the right moment has always appeared. The challenge is to know what the right signs are and you can only do that if you practice being open to receive it.

For me, being physically active, emotionally aware and spiritually open to seeing the 'messages' is crucial. I have found in my experience, the answer to any question is usually staring me right in the face. What I have learnt is often the solution was actually not as I thought. It was exactly what I needed/wanted/ desired but often it didn't come the way I thought it would.

Dealing with David's issues as they arose, then trying to sort out what was going on for him at any given time, forced me to rely on my intuition to get to the bottom of the issue and then to create the solution. I had to be sure I knew exactly what I wanted and then to ask for it as clearly and as specifically as I could. Not to ask for what I didn't want.

David didn't have fluent verbal skills to explain what was happening to him or describe a situation he was stressed about, so it was up to me, as his mother, to put up the "radar,"; to ask the right questions, and then figure it out. I was the language he couldn't speak, and I needed to use my intuition to make sense of the stress he was feeling.

For instance, while I would be asking David questions, I would also be replaying situations or conversations in my head that perhaps would give me a clue. The conversation or situation may have happened yesterday, two weeks ago, or a month ago and sometimes what had happened was not even related to what the real issue was. But by relying on my intuition, I was able to guide the conversation to get to the bottom line.

It was up to me to be open, to look for the answer, and then recognize it when it materialized. Sometimes I needed to be told or shown the answer several times and several ways before I actually got it…but when I got it—it often blew me away. It could have been something staring me in the face for ages, and it wasn't until I connected the 'dots' that it all made sense. I became like an investigative detective, pulling all the pieces together to create the solution. The more I opened myself up to the ability to ask the right questions and listen to my own intuitive answers, the easier the solutions became.

Physical, emotional, spiritual and intuitive fitness go hand in hand. They give you the strength to be patient, they give you the strength to be understanding, and they give you the strength to stop and take a breath when the challenges all become too hard.

Physical, emotional, spiritual, and intuitive fitness won't make the challenges go away, but they will give you the strength to deal with the challenges that arise.

LESSONS LEARNED THROUGH FAILURE

For the first few years after the diagnosis, I read every book, visited every Web site, and attended every seminar I could find on the subject of Asperger's syndrome.

I held in my head the belief that if I became an expert, I could fix this. I was David's champion, and in that role, I would make it better: talk to teachers, find friends, and sit over him at night endlessly explaining what he did not understand. I took on the mantle of the "saviour," and if I couldn't find a cure, then I was certainly going to make things right.

When I came down with glandular fever, it was, as I realized later, the wake-up call I needed. All of a sudden, I was just too tired to fix things. I was too exhausted and depleted of energy. I had simply come to the end of my tether.

But while I was recuperating, I slowly came to realize that my beliefs had caused the illness. I believed that the world rested on my shoulders; I believed that it was up to me to fix this; and I believed the success and happiness of the family depended on me! No wonder I got sick!

As I began the process of recovery, I knew I had to hand everybody's life back to them. I couldn't be all things to all people and have a healthy relationship with them.

It was then I made the decision to step out of David's life and let him live his own life. That didn't mean I would abandon him, nor would I stop being a part of his life; it was just I wasn't going to run it for him.

I realized that if he was going to learn how to navigate life, then I needed to step aside and walk with him, rather than pushing him from behind or pulling him from the front.

I stopped focusing on dealing with a child who had Asperger's syndrome and instead focus on raising a young man who saw things differently.

I was not here to rescue David; I was here to guide him. I was not here to fight his battles for him; I was here to watch and wait and help him decide what was worth fighting for. I was not here to be dominant in his life; I was here to be a support in his life. I was not here to make life better for him; I was here to help him become a strong, self-directed individual who knew the right strategies to create a better life for himself.

The subtle differences in the wording made all the difference. It was so freeing for me. At the same time, I watched David emerge as a confident young man in the process.

I was there for him then, and I am still there; however, for the most part, I let him find his own way. It hasn't always been a smooth road and he still makes mistakes along the way, just like any neurotypical young person, but at least they are his own mistakes, with the pain and the learning that comes from discovering his own truth in the mistakes and his own path in the learning.

We have a saying in our house—there are far greater lessons in failure than in success. You have more to gain when you fail. It simply becomes a series of questions is this important to me? If it is, then what do I need to do to become better at it? If it's not important, fine move on—it wasn't meant to be anyway.

Children with Asperger's syndrome need to experience failure, because that's how they learn and understand how to get it right or do it better—just like anybody else. However, sometimes, I let David's difference get in the way of him experiencing every facet of his life. I spent too much time shielding him from the pain of failure because sometimes it seemed that he never experienced success. And right in that space, between success and failure, was the key. I had to be whole and present to know exactly where the line could be drawn and know the difference between the two.

For the last eight years, I have worked in the school system. I have seen many parents defend their child when the child has done something wrong or argue with teachers, taking sides with their child, when it is obvious that their child was at fault. I have seen parents do their child's project or assignment, make excuses for them if they hand in an assignment late, or rush to school with forgotten homework so their child won't get into trouble. I have witnessed parents challenging teachers or sport coaches if their child doesn't win an award they feel they are deserving of. As a result, I have seen many children who have absolutely no sense of who they are. They are unable or unwilling to accept responsibility for their own actions and worst of all become totally ignorant of what it takes to be successful or a whole person, all because they have never been able to experience what it is like to learn their own lessons.

As hard as it is as a parent to watch your children fail, or miss out, or get into trouble, these are also the greatest lessons you can give. Children cannot and should not be protected from failure, because through failure we learn. As parents, the buffer you set up and the attitude you take to help your child learn through the experience of failure makes all the difference.

For David, if he did something that was not acceptable, then we needed to find another way of doing it. If his math results were not as good as he thought, then we would sit down and figure out what he didn't understand—yet! It was up to us as parents to guide that failure to find the success.

Failure doesn't mean you are stupid. Failure means you didn't get it right the first time. Failure does not make you any less of a person; in fact, it actually molds and develops character and focus. Accepting failure as simply a learning experience gives you the knowledge to know how to do it right the next time. Failure is not personal. It is a situation, and how you view it becomes a choice.

Life is not always about being right or always being successful. Each time you fail, what you learn in the process takes you one step closer to getting it right the next time. Helping David understand failure, allowed us to accept the failure we had experienced in our own lives had gotten us to the point where we are now. And you know what? Each time we failed, we actually did it better the next time and really, it wasn't that bad after all!

SIMPLICITY

Recently, Caitlin and I found a whole box of old videotapes taken right through our "dark" period, as I thought it was.

When we sold our house, all the profits had to go to paying off some of the bills we had created during the end of the real estate boom. Although we made some profit allowing us to pay back the bank, my father, and our credit card bills, little was left over for anything else, and for many years, the bills continued to pile up.

The old house we moved into was huge in comparison to the house we had owned, triple in size in fact. We had little furniture: an old lounge suit, an old dining setting, and an outdoor setting we used for a "formal" dining suite.

We lived in this huge house with little furniture, and at the time, I always felt it signified our lives: big and empty without a lot of ourselves in it!

But, in viewing these tapes, I realized the little furniture we had actually allowed us to do so many things. I ran seminars in our front living room and three times a week held morning aerobics classes—yes, it was that big!

The other surprise after watching the videos, was the realization of how free the children were in that house. Without furniture to block paths, they learned to dance and roller skate and played all sorts of dress-up and imaginary games. They had the freedom to be unrestricted and live totally in their imagination.

We had a pool, where they spent an enormous amount of time. In watching the videos, I remembered that Caitlin had learned to swim in four days and that David and Alissa were entertained for hours on end with all sorts of games they made up in and around the pool.

During that time, the swimming, the imaginary games, and the freedom all helped David to learn skills that have helped him throughout his life.

Swimming was an excellent way in which he improved his motor skills, coordination, imagination, strength, and getting along with others.

The imaginary games taught him how to interact with others and create fascinating stories to act out. He didn't like reading, but he loved making up plays and games he, Alissa, and Caitlin could play together. He loved the freedom to explore his inner world, uninterrupted by rules. His imagination, so honed in those years, now helps him to make films and devise stories in a career he now wants to pursue.

The simplicity of his childhood, which was not cluttered with objects and restrictions but still consisted of routines and structure, allowed him time to sort situations out in his head. He felt safe with the routines and structures we created, which allowed him to feel free to explore his world through his imagination. I can look back now on his childhood and see how the situations we were placed in at the time actually created the best outcomes for him.

When we didn't have any money to do what other families could do, we actually created a simple, free life, allowing the children to grow up with wonderful imaginations and a sense of freedom. They were happy with the simple things of life. They were happy to take a boogie board and turn it into a boat or a plane or a place for a picnic in the middle of the pool. They were happy to take sheets from the cupboard, chairs from the dining room, and pillows from the beds to create a fort in the middle of the lounge room, serving afternoon tea to imaginary friends.

They were happy to make up plays and dances and to put on shows for us, which are very interesting to look back on now since all three children are involved in the arts in some way.

Even though it looked like we were doing without, we were perhaps one of the wealthiest families I knew!

CONNECTING WITH NATURE

Having a child with Asperger's syndrome is challenging for all members of the family, and hence, we looked for many opportunities to spend time with just our family, creating activities as stress free as possible for all of us.

We spent most weekends on our own because it was often too difficult if we went anywhere with other families. David didn't cope well when other people were around so picnics became our release. Weekends were always spent at a park, on the beach or in the rainforest somewhere.

Sundays, we were always up early, out of the house by 9am and at our favorite picnic spots somewhere, by 10am, not coming home until late in the afternoon.

Asperger's children need to have regular contact with nature away from suburbia and all it entails.

Those with Asperger's are not the only ones who need a break from the extraneous noise and electrical energy coming from TV, computers, or music through iPods. Many people now live their lives surrounded by noise and electrical stimulation from either working on a computer, listening to music, or watching TV.

Because we could actually see and gauge the rise in David's stress level when he was constantly surrounded by people, computers, or TV, when we connected with nature, we saw the difference in him almost straight away. It became very obvious whenever we missed one of our weekend "retreats" because issues often arose during the week.

Alternatively, the days spent out with nature created a gentle, healing quality that calmed the stress and created a sense of peace. This became a very important tool for us, but also David guided it.

We would spend many Sunday's bushwalking, trying to teach the children about the birds or trees. David mostly ignored any of our attempts to get him involved with learning about the flora and fauna of a particular area. But although he didn't always seem to be participating, the sheer experience of connecting with the trees and the earth and the many birds and animals existing in the rainforest or the bush helped him ground his frenetic energy.

There didn't always appear there were inroads, and I can remember being frustrated because he wouldn't learn about trees. But he used to make up games in the trunks and roots of the trees. So his connection with the energy was in essence helping him to ground his energy levels and opening his ability to learn.

The beach and the ocean for David were also particularly cathartic. We had lived on the beach since David was a baby, so he had grown up listening to the ocean and playing in (and eating) the sand. Many autistic children react adversely to sand, but this was not the case with David.

He loved the ocean and swimming in the salt water. To this day, when we go to the beach, he will spend hours body surfing or just allowing the ocean waves to wash over him. Again, the gift of the ocean and the connection with the purity of the salt, sand, and air ground him and seem to allow him to open his own heart to a connection he has to the ocean.

Spending time in these places just as a family was important. When others came with us, although it was fun, it became incredibly stressful for David. When we, as a family, allowed him to be himself, without any expectations or interruptions by others, he could connect with the natural world. If we stepped in and tried to get him to look at the birds, to read the information on the sign and learn something, the magic was lost. Allowing him to absorb his own messages from nature seemed to relax and de-stress him, not us trying to force it on him.

Today, this becomes even more essential for us all. We have created a tradition for Mother's Day, Father's Day, and birthdays, in which we have told our children that we would much prefer their presence, rather than their presents, on those days. So while we look forward to the opportunity to get all of us together in one spot, we also take the opportunity to relive some of the traditions we had when they were small.

Picnics are still a favorite pastime, and that connection for us as a family, grounded within a natural environment, reaps amazing benefits for all of us, with noticeable energy differences. These picnics have become an essential tradition in surviving our busy, involved lives.

As with many of the tools we discovered that would work for David, we have found the connection with nature and silence one of the greatest tools for all of us. We very seldom watch TV, only if there is a program we all want to watch. We are more likely to come home from work, light some incense and candles, put on some great jazz or mellow music, and spend hours around the dinner table talking.

Calm and peace create space for you to find solutions to any dilemma or challenge. I have seen this firsthand because of what we had to do to create a stress-free environment for David. But again, through the gift of having David in our lives, we have created solutions that work for all sorts of challenges and for the whole family.

THE OTHER LANGUAGE

From years of observing David, I have truly come to understand something, and that is the "other language" that occurs in the mind of a child with Asperger's syndrome. I often used the phrase "it's like he comes from another planet." He saw things differently than we did, heard words differently than we did, and saw situations and experiences totally differently than the way we did.

In our quiet bean-bag times, often I would have to explain, in many different ways, a question he had asked. It was as if I had to find the common language or variation of the language that would make sense to him. I have dealt with many children with Asperger's syndrome over the years, and I have found this to be true for them as well. Not all language is the same, but usually the misinterpretation of the meaning of words can cause many concerns. Whilst the language many children with Asperger's use is very literal, even then, they often tend to use the same word to describe many different emotions.

Sometimes it would take many attempts to find commonality in the language used. This, for David, was a source of much of his frustration. He often found it difficult to grasp the meaning of words others took for granted. For instance, if somebody asked him to stand "over there" he found it incredibly frustrating because "over there" was not specific enough for him; or asking him to "wait on a minute" would drive him crazy – because a minute meant a minute —not three minutes or five minutes.

This led to extreme frustration as the language people often used didn't make sense in his world. Through this, Gerry and I got used to saying what we mean and meaning what we said. We stopped using generalizations and had to really think about the essence of the words we used, as much as their meanings.

Although in the beginning this was challenging, we became very used to not assuming anything and checking with David to make sure he understood what we meant. To this day, I still find myself going over and over in my mind the words I use to describe something to make sure it makes sense. But I also realized that many people say things that are misinterpreted. How often have you been in a situation where somebody has said something to you and you have taken it out of context? Having a child with Asperger's just makes you all the more aware of the 'other language' that often masks what we truly mean to say.

Making it all Work

Challenging behaviors will arise at all times, depending on the age of the child with Asperger's syndrome. Sometimes they can be few and far between, and sometimes they can seem to happen with such astounding regularity, you wonder where all that energy comes from!

When David became upset about something it was essential that I remained calm so I could feel, intuitively, what was going on.

The first step was to breathe, and check that I was in a place where I could deal with the emotion effectively and with compassion. (I didn't always get it right, but it was the plan!). The second step was to remember one simple truth— this reaction to whatever is happening is the difference he is trying to live with. So when he did react, I would remind myself that he did so because he didn't know how else to respond. It was a more powerful place to be and kept the frustration levels down.

Next, I would get down onto his level so I could look him in the eye or at least so I was not looking down at him. I would ask him to look at me. Sometimes he looked at me, but sometimes he looked in the general vicinity of where I was standing. It depended on how stressed he was. Sometimes, depending on what was happening, I needed to move David away from the noise or the situation, so whatever was going on was not creating more angst.

To help, I created key phrases I would say all the time so he knew this was serious. It was his key to understand we were going to have a mum-and son talk!

I had three phrases that I used depending on the situation.

"David, what you just did was inappropriate."

"I can see you are upset; explain to me what happened."

"What are you feeling right now?"

By asking questions about what had happened and about what he was feeling helped him connect with his own emotions and, by doing so, learn to understand them.

It took time and an extraordinary amount of patience and, many times, great intuitive detective work, but right in the moment, I had the opportunity to create the distinction and figure out what was going on. I would keep reminding myself that he responded the way he did because he didn't know how else to react.

It was during these times, I had to learn to open up my heart to hear what David's heart was saying, because often the words he used, and the feelings he had, didn't make any logical sense. Sometimes he was responding to something that could have happened five minutes ago, five hours ago, or five days ago, and this incident, whatever it was, had triggered a reaction. In David's case, it could sometimes take hours to figure out what it was. But one thing I learned to be absolutely true was that there was always a reason behind the behavior, always.

Nothing in the mind of a child with Asperger's is random, although it may appear that way. A sudden violent reaction to something somebody says or does, an inappropriate rage in a supermarket when there are five people standing at each checkout, or a totally unexplainable meltdown to something that appears to be relatively minor is linked to something that has happened.

It is only through the heart connection, I could get it, because it often didn't make sense in my head. When I connected on that level, from his heart to my heart, he responded.

212

After we got through that, the next was to help him to understand the emotion and his response so he would learn from that emotion.

"I can see/sense/understand why that makes you feel frustrated/angry/upset; that was unkind/must be stressful/must make you angry."

Many call this stage proactive listening; I just call it compassion!

David dealt with many people at school and throughout his life who had absolutely no idea why he reacted the way he did to a situation. I wanted to create a bond with him so he knew that anywhere, at anytime, somebody in his world whom he knew he could trust would help him navigate the world, and that person was his mother.

During this time, I would also look or sense what was going on around him at the time. Was the music too loud? Were people moving quickly, making loud noises? Did something happen two days ago, when I picked him up from school that was a little "hmm" moment that hadn't made sense to me at the time?

Did he say something recently that made me think he didn't understand somebody's actions? Every reaction has a reason; when you can see through the behavior, you will see the reason for the behavior.

Depending on what was going on for David and where he was along the path to understanding, I would then give options for him to learn a different response. Again, they were not always the same but were based on my sense of what was occurring.

"Perhaps the next time that happens, a better response would be to go for a walk or say, 'No, I don't like it when you do that.'" Or if it happened at school, I would say, "Did you tell the teacher, 'I am really stressed at the present time, because I don't understand what you are saying.'"

Or, if we had been down this path before and I knew we had created a better strategy, I would ask, "What do you think would have been a better response?"

However, I wouldn't use the last strategy unless I knew we had been down this path before, because if I questioned David about how he should have responded differently and he did not know how to answer the question, his stress level would rise even further.

As I learned the hard way, if he knew a better way to respond, then he would have done it! There was no one way to approach an issue, because the people or situations were often different. Most neurotypical people can take a when-this-happens, then-do-this response and can figure out how to use the knowledge in different situations. But that didn't create solutions for David because he had difficulty transposing the scenarios. Not all bullying situations were the same in his head; not all stress-intensifying situations were the same. Each circumstance was different, and so often we would have to break each situation down and analyze the emotions and the responses.

However, once the light went on for him and he got the distinction of the differences or similarities in each situation, then he could normally put the response into practice. The not knowing how to react created the stress and the inappropriate behaviors.

I have also learned to use these skills for all sorts of situations: in dealing with an angry or sad parent or client, in dealing with the challenges of puberty with both my daughters, and in getting the right outcome to a negative situation.

There are so many times when people don't say what it is they really mean: when "I am angry" really means "I am frustrated or sad," when "I hate you" really means "I don't understand what is happening to me," and when a slammed door really means "I am tired and I am so overwhelmed."

I have used the same strategies with my daughters whenever I could sense something was going on in their lives. In most circumstances, an angry outburst or a door-slamming incident usually meant something was going on that needed to be talked through.

214

Compassion, love, patience, and understanding are the only "skills" you need to solve most situations. I had always thought I was a patient person; it wasn't until I had a child with Asperger's syndrome that I truly valued each syllable and nuance in the word *patient* and that I learned to truly enjoy the value of a glass of wine!

ROUTINES AND AGREEMENTS

R outines create safety, and they create success. In all aspects of life, creating a routine gives you guidelines to help you achieve the goals you have in life.

If you want to get fit, you have to set up a routine to work out each day. If you want to have a successful sales career, routine is essential in making sure you are making a certain amount of phone calls each day. In order to write this book, I had to create a routine to give myself the time and freedom to spend at the computer each day to ensure it would be completed. Just wishing and wanting the book to be written were not going to get the words on paper! Success in any business, or in any sport for that matter, is focusing on goals and then each day sticking to routines in order to move closer to those goals.

A household with an Asperger's child works exactly the same way. The routine of the day allows the child to feel safe, and as the routine becomes easier and more accepted, then within those routines, you can add small changes or strategies to reach the next level of success.

I didn't truly understand the value and the purpose of a routine until I could evaluate just how powerful routine was in helping David feel safe and confident. Punctuality was crucial in David's world. If I said that I was going to pick him up from school at 3:15, then 3:15 it had to be—not 3:20, not 3:25, but 3:15. If I were stuck in traffic, for instance, and I could see him waiting for me to pick him up and he hadn't yet seen my car, I could actually see him becoming more and more agitated with each minute past 3:15 he waited.

Sometimes it was annoying and sometimes frustrating but now, many years later, I can see why the routine was so important for him.

Routines allowed David to feel safe in a world that felt very unsafe. For children with Asperger's syndrome being adaptable is not in their nature; it is something they must learn.

At the school where I worked, the parents of a young boy with Asperger's were constantly late, not one or two minutes, but by as much as thirty minutes, or sometimes an hour or more. I could see him from my office window, watching as his stress levels rose. It was heartbreaking. Many times, I would go out to the school grounds to ask him if he wanted to come into my office to phone his parents, and after a while he would come in almost every day to call them. After he had spoken to them, he would walk out of my office complaining about how frustrating parents were and why people just don't do as they say! To expect a child with Asperger's to simply accept lateness is just not appropriate; it doesn't it fit into their world.

Creating routines and making and keeping agreements are about trust. When I made a statement, David knew he could trust me, could trust me to do as I said, could trust me to be there to pick him up when I said I would, could trust if he needed me I would always be there, and, most of all, could trust that he was important in my world. It was the basis of a great relationship. By me helping him create a routine, he also learned that making and keeping agreements is important.

In dealing with others, being on time and keeping agreements are crucial to creating trust. Excuses just don't cut the mustard. Learning to keep agreements will help with any behavioral program you set up for your children and will create trust with those who you deal with on a work basis. People will trust you if you keep your agreements, and routines help you get there.

For you as a caregiver, being punctual and keeping those agreements may not seem important, especially when you have other children or your own job to contend with, because you can easily justify all sorts of issues in a rational way. For a child with Asperger's their difference doesn't allow that.

These days, since David is older, there are no issues with time. If we are held up for any reason (and thank goodness for mobile phones), David is quite prepared to adapt and understand the reason for the lateness. But it is because we spent years cultivating trust, which in turn has laid the framework for him also to learn trustworthiness and honesty in relationships he creates with others. He values honesty and knows that when you make an agreement or arrangement with somebody, then you must honor that agreement —a very valuable lesson for all people, not just those with Asperger's.

CREATING FAMILIAR RITUALS

When the children were little, we would insist everybody sat down for dinner together every night, and the TV was turned off. We lit candles (still do) and played soft calming music. The candles came about as we found the bright lights tended to take David's focus away. By lighting candles, he kept his focus on the candles, and they became quite cathartic for him.

We insisted the table was set in the appropriate manner, with napkins, water jugs, good cutlery, and crockery, and each night was a formal occasion. It didn't matter about the time; it was when we all were home together. All the children knew, unless Gerry was going to be late and had advised us earlier, then when he came home, that's when we had dinner.

Each of the children had a job: set the table, pour water in the glasses, and so on. Nobody was allowed to start dinner until both Gerry and I were sitting. Each night everybody got to talk about his or her day and one good thing that happened.

Now within this routine, we would constantly say quietly to David, *"Turn around, David"; "Use your knife and fork, David"; "Sit up straight, David."* Or, often, I would just reach over, grab his hand, and turn him so he was facing us all, because it was so easy for him to lose his focus.

And those years of dinner-table routine have paid off. The night of David's graduation from the Technical College, my father took us all out for dinner. The waiter brought out all the meals, and my father, who was sitting at the head of the table, was last to get his meal. All of the children sat and waited until Dad picked up his fork before they started on their meals. And all of the children spoke in turn, asking each other questions, interspersed with lots of laughter and good-natured banter. A gentleman, who was sitting at the table next to me, stopped me on the way out and complimented us on the fine manners our children exhibited.

To this day, my children possess this habit, which I am exceptionally proud of. Each of them knows exactly what to do at a dinner table, how to put their knives and forks down between bites, how to lay their knife and fork out when they are finished, and they never leave the table without asking to be excused.

The routine of our family dinners gave David, especially, the knowledge and ability to be able to converse with people in one of the most socially acceptable environments—the dinner table. Many people have commented to us on David's exceptional manners and etiquette at the table. But it did not come about through us just telling him what to do. It was a routine we established, and it took many years to become a part of his world.

That is the value of routine. We never wavered from what we expected at the dinner table. Although some nights could be frustrating, especially if we were tired there were often times when we would have preferred just sit in front of the TV and not communicate. But the outcome of that routine has been so rewarding and has given David and our daughters a valuable gift. I wonder sometimes whether we would have been so insistent on the routine had we not had Asperger's in our lives. It's a question I will probably never know the answer to.

OUR JOURNEY

In my quiet moments, I often reflect on the journey we have taken as a family. During the writing of this book and the rereading of my journals, I was so overwhelmed with many of the memories I had totally forgotten about. I must admit to actually smiling and feeling a great sense of satisfaction in what we have managed to achieve since those very dark days.

One Sunday evening, after I had been writing all day, I walked down stairs and poured two glasses of wine. I handed one to Gerry and sat at the kitchen bench while he was preparing dinner and said, "I can't believe we survived. I had forgotten just how far we have really come!" I was totally overwhelmed in realizing just what we had been through and how we were still together as a family, let alone as a couple. If somebody had told me 10 years ago, that this is where we would be now —I would never have believed them! The reality of what we had been through hit me all of a sudden. I actually couldn't find words to adequately describe the overwhelming emotion.

Many years ago, I heard a story that perhaps best describes the impact of finding out your child has Asperger's syndrome. The story describes planning a trip to France. How you plan to visit the Eiffel Tower, the Arc de Triomphe, and look forward to enjoying French wine and cuisine. But, after you board the plane, the pilot suddenly announces you are, in fact, about to land in the Netherlands.

At first, you are disappointed, angry, and despairing because the whole trip was planned to enjoy France. But after landing in the Netherlands, you fall in love with the tulips, the windmills, and the wonderful Dutch food, and you realize there were just as many wonderful things to experience in the Netherlands as there are in France. The moral of the story simply is although the trip you end up taking wasn't what you had planned, the experience was amazing!

Having a child who has Asperger's, or any difference, is just the same experience. It's not what you planned, but the experience is extraordinary. The gifts your child brings to your life, and his or her ability to touch emotions you never imagined you had, or knew could be so intense, gives your life such depth and meaning.

You can think you have experienced pain, you can think you had experienced anger and frustration and despair and loneliness, and you can think you knew what love was all about, but nothing quite prepares you for this. Whilst coming to terms with all those emotions, many people also have to deal with the judgment and opinions of others. Many parents tell me they feel simply overwhelmed by this experience; describing how tired they get; how sad they feel, how stressful each day becomes because they are constantly on guard, watching and waiting for the moment when things will unravel. However most of all many truly grieve for their loss of normality.

Asperger's syndrome is not a reservation for one. It is not just about the child, this difference is about the whole family. It can tear relationships apart and drive wedges between family members. It can place stress on the siblings who often watch in silence as their brother or sister has a meltdown, while they struggle to be noticed. Through all of this, their parents work to truly make life normal for everyone.

There is a part of the heart of a parent going through this that nobody will ever know. It is that place where you know that in your darkest hour, your anger can cause harm; where despair can cause emotions that are overwhelming. It is that place where the loneliness and heartbreak are palpable and immeasurable in their darkness and grief. At the same time, your protectiveness can only be compared to a mother bear prepared to fight to the death against men armed with guns!

But the opposite is also true: it is also the place where joy and love exist with emotion words cannot describe. The first time your child looks straight into your heart and you know you have connected; the first time your child walks, smiles, writes a word or tells a story, even though that milestone maybe many months or years behind other children. Such small, measurable, much anticipated and desired milestones can make so many months of frustration suddenly become worth it.

While having a child of difference can be challenging, it is also a gift, because you truly do come to the essence of parenting. This child will force you to soul search continually for the true meaning of life, and because of that your priorities change.

The lesson we learned from David and the gift he has given us as parents is simple. In order for us to help David to become who he needed to be, we needed to become the people we wanted him to be.

In order to be the most effective parents possible, we had to be totally honest with ourselves. We had to clearly understand our own beliefs, thought patterns, expectations, judgments, and emotions. But most of all we had open up our hearts and parent from the heart first. However, in order to do that, we had to first be courageous enough to wade deep into the abyss of our sadness and grief and come to terms with the fact that we were sad, we were grieving and that was OK. Denying those feelings only made it worse. When we confronted them, accepted them and dealt with them, that's when things really changed for us.

The amount of raw emotion flowing through our house in those early days was impossible to sustain without something breaking. Our marriage, our health, and the well-being of our two daughters were just as important as helping David come to terms with Asperger's.

There were a number of things in our lives that we decided to change, and in doing so, the flow-on effect in David's life was obvious. So when we made the decision to work on ourselves and on our relationship, we helped David to understand love and relationships; When we made the decision to understand our own emotions and beliefs, we allowed David to discover his own emotions and beliefs and to understand them; By creating routine and being willing to make and keep meaningful agreements, we taught David how to trust and how to be trustworthy; When we decided to trust and to be guided by our intuition, we also gave David permission to trust and be guided by his intuition; And when we decided to be resilient and compassionate and to change our language to reflect what we wanted in our lives, resilience, compassion and empowering language also became a part of David's life.

But those decisions were not just about David; those decisions also had a great impact on our two daughters. We wanted to raise them to be independent young women, intelligent, compassionate, and caring— knowing that they could dream and achieve whatever they wanted to achieve.

Having a brother with a difference was not an excuse for them not to experience all they needed to experience. Rather, it was the opportunity for them to learn how to be grateful for what they have and to find a sense of purpose in their own lives. I am very proud of how our two daughters have become self-directed young women who are on their own paths to success. They are sensitive, empathetic, and extremely intolerant of those who bully, judge, or mistreat others. They stand up for those they feel are the underdogs and will not allow in their circle of friends those who abuse themselves or others.

For Gerry and I, the journey has been exhilarating to say the least. We have now been together over thirty years and still spend much of our time developing who we are, learning more about the human condition, and taking time to explore the talents we bring to the world.

Toward the end of 2000, things changed dramatically for us, both personally and financially. During that time, we both found careers that allowed us to not only enjoy going to work every day but that also created financial security.

We are both able to look back on that period in our lives, when we felt as though the wheels had fallen off, as actually an incredibly valuable and spiritual shift in our roles as parents. For me especially, where once I had thought I had failed because I had not been successful in my chosen career, I now realize that giving up on that career for a period of time, allowed me to achieve the one goal that was truly important to me — helping David to get through those years of struggle, to emerge to where he is today. As I evolved during that time, the way that I parent and the way that I live my life changed. As a woman, wife and mother I am still evolving, but within each stage of evolvement comes more wisdom and authenticity. In my travels and speaking engagements now I have come across so many other mothers who say exactly the same thing. That this child of difference has come into their lives and because of that their lives have changed so profoundly, so much so they don't even recognize who they were before. In the fractious times, I know many yearn for a time when life was simpler, but most value the gifts that their child has bought to their lives and are able to laugh at those whose problems seem so simple in comparison.

When I decided that the buck really stopped with me, that's when everything changed. I learned that I needed to become whole and aim to live only in the present. This was important not only for David, but also for my daughters. It was critical that I stopped thinking about what could have been, or spend time worrying about things that may or may not happen in the future. Instead I needed to 'live in the question', and focus on creating empowering solutions to issues as they arose. At the same time I needed to remind myself to rejoice and celebrate each milestone and achievement no matter how small.

It is quite ironic that 10 years after I walked away from my career as a writer and seminar presenter, that I am now back doing the same thing— but this time it is just so much better. I had passion and conviction for what I wrote about and taught before, but this time; I have peeled back all the layers of the onion and I am now here as a complete and whole person, living fully in the present moment, sharing my story to help others find solutions in their journey.

David's gift to us was to aspire to be greater parents than we thought possible. David's gift to his sisters was to help them become amazing, compassionate young women, who believe nothing stands in their way of achieving exactly what they want to achieve and he is a constant source of inspiration to them (albeit sometimes annoying and frustrating!).

Somebody once asked me if I could imagine what our life would have been like if David didn't have Asperger's syndrome. For a minute I imagined how much simpler and easier our lives would have been. Then I thought about who we had become as individuals and who we have become as a family.

It was then I realized, that as painful and difficult as this journey has been, Asperger's syndrome actually challenged us, confronted us and inspired us to become the people, and the family, we are today… it truly was David's gift to us.

JUST ABOUT ASPERGER'S SYNDROME

In the following pages, some of the strategies we have used to help us, and David, come to terms with living with Asperger's syndrome are detailed. This section of the book is specifically for parents dealing with the challenges that arise in trying to understand this difference. However, some of the strategies may be able to assist you if you are dealing with challenging behaviors from neurotypical children as well.

INSIDE ASPERGER'S SYNDROME

Asperger's syndrome (or autism spectrum disorders) can be difficult to understand. Those diagnosed are often very intelligent people, it's just they do some rather unique things and often have unusual ways of interrelating with people.

Most people diagnosed with Asperger's have similar traits: most are intelligent and often are very knowledgeable on a particular subject. They have incredible focus in their area of interest and, if faced with a challenge, will maintain that focus while being totally oblivious of time, hunger, coldness, tiredness, or outside influences. Because they have the ability to be totally immersed in a specific subject for long periods, without the need to be distracted by things/people/situations, they can often achieve amazing success in life—once they are allowed to be totally immersed in their particular area of interest.

Many of the world's greatest and most successful explorers, inventors, engineers, scientists, doctors, musicians, directors, actors and computer software developers have Asperger's-like tendencies.

However, because of this intense ability to focus, they can often be quite blunt in ignoring or dismissing those who they see as not as intelligent as they are. They find socialization difficult, and they can appear to be distant, antisocial, cold, and uncaring, when in fact a person with Asperger's can be very lonely. In most cases, they truly do long for good friendships and a sense of belonging; it's just they don't understand how to make them.

They don't understand why others are not fascinated in their particular area of interest and often find small talk or social chit chat boring. Many find background noise frustrating, so will avoid social 'scenes' such as parties or gatherings where a large number of people congregate.

As a person with Asperger's moves through life and finds their own way to express their talents, the need for socialization and acceptance often becomes less intense. They often find likeminded people to associate with as they move into careers they love.

However, during the early childhood and adolescence years, the challenges of this diagnosis are intense and heartbreaking as parents struggle to find the balance in understanding the diagnosis at the different ages and stages.

The early years are often a whirlwind of emotion and discovery, including early intervention strategies, appointments with different specialists, negotiating with schools and teachers, and dealing with the judgment of other parents, and sometimes other family members.

The next step is navigating the teenage years a time when parents have to help their child move to acceptance and self determination. The teenage years are a tough time for most young people as they struggle with peer group dynamics. For a child with Asperger's syndrome, this time is often particularly difficult as they truly begin to see that they are different; when the 'tribe' mentality of the middle years of high school truly kicks in; when those who are different are more likely to be excluded from the pecking order of the teenage social group. This is the time when children with Asperger's are particularly susceptible to bullying, taunting and loneliness. Because those with Asperger's often look just like everyone else, are often intelligent, and can appear to be very able-bodied, their responses are often considered odd or unacceptable. This leaves them open to being shunned by their peers and misunderstood by others.

When somebody is physically disabled, we actually see it. We see the person in a wheelchair or using a walker who cannot navigate stairs or access small toilets. It still must be so incredibly frustrating for those with a physical disability to not have access to so many things many take for granted. But as a community, we are slowly working toward greater understanding of physical disabilities. But because the disability is so visual, just like many situations in life, we have learned to accept that which is staring us in the face.

Because Asperger's syndrome often presents no physical differences, people make judgments about children's behavior. Because it is not an obvious "disability" but rather is a difference in the way they interact with the world, assumptions that they are "putting it on" or that they are "being difficult or naughty" are made.

Those with Asperger's syndrome are often extremely sensitive to various stimuli. Things such as noise, cold, heat, the feel of certain clothing, the smell of certain environments, the lighting in certain buildings, or crowded environments could all be trigger points for a meltdown or inappropriate response.

At the same time, they often have difficulty in explaining what is actually causing the stress, which can then intensify to an even more potentially explosive situation, as people try to fix what is going or try to understand it. The constant questions and comments are often met with intense frustration. So many times, David would be extremely upset about something, and every time I asked him a question, he would become even more frustrated as we (or I) tried to sort out what was really going on. It was those times that I would have to truly draw on every ounce of my patience and my intuition to try and diffuse the situation and create an alternative strategy.

I have often imagined living with Asperger's to be like traveling to a very different country, a country where the language, the customs, the alphabet, the food, the terrain, the climate, and the people are incredibly different from what we are used to.

Did you know that if you travel to Mongolia for instance, when you enter a ger, a home of the Mongolian nomads, you do not step on the threshold? Usually, guests move in a clockwise direction when entering the ger, first to the west and then north. (Ger doors always face south.) The east side of the ger (on your right as you enter) is normally where the family will sit, and the west side (on your left as you enter) is for guests. Food and cooking implements are stored on the right side, or the women's side of the ger, and saddles, bridles, and things associated with men's work on the left, or the men's side.

When I read about those customs, I could imagine that I would be incredibly stressed by trying to figure out which way was west and which way was east, let alone trying to remember which side was which!

Those with Asperger's syndrome live their lives every day trying to remember strange customs of the neurotypical world. And what is worse is that, often, those customs change, depending on who is dictating the custom. Those with Asperger's constantly come across people who do not understand why they act the way they do. They live in a world that embraces normalcy, which really means conformity. It's just in their world; conformity doesn't make sense at all.

For the parents, living with a child with Asperger's syndrome can be heartbreaking because although there are many similarities in the diagnosis, there are also many variances, requiring many different strategies, rather than simply a textbook set of rules.

Because the child with Asperger's syndrome is struggling to understand this "other" planet, he or she demands more from their parents than other children do. The parents become the only people the child can trust to help him or her learn what the child needs to learn, and for some parents, the burden can be astounding or overwhelming.

Children with Asperger's insist that you, as their parent, are constantly aware of their surroundings so you can pre-empt any potentially stressful situations, because they will react to outside stimuli way before others do. They demand you understand their inner motives, forcing you to go beneath the surface and delve deeply into the workings of their mind.

They expect you to be authentic, truthful, and honest because that is how they make sense of their world, and they demand that you adhere to routines, make and keep agreements, and, above all, love them unconditionally—all the time.

They need you to be confident, optimistic, insightful, and resilient. When you have another focus, when you are not understanding of their needs, and when you are not true to yourself, that's when they react.

It is as if, as a parent, you have to become more of and clearer on every aspect of emotional humanness so that your Asperger's child can figure out human emotions.

We neurotypicals don't keep agreements. We don't say and do what we mean. We change our minds and think it's OK. We set a goal to do something, then get caught up with a phone call, an e-mail, or a conversation and don't get around to completing what we set out to do. We use vague language often with double meanings. We break road rules—just a little over the speed limit or not coming to a complete stop at the stop sign— and make it OK because everybody does it.

The person diagnosed with Asperger's has to learn all of these socially acceptable nuances of life, which have no written-down rules. This is incredibly frustrating for them, as their world has a rigid set of black and white boundaries, with very few gray areas.

David did not set out to act inappropriately, nor did we, as a family, allow him to misbehave. But when placed in a stressful situation, he would act in whatever manner he felt was appropriate. We had to create a certain set of responses, repeat them, and not diverge from those so the appropriate response could eventually become second nature to him.

A different behavior sets a pattern. Once the new, learned pattern was in place, the next one became easier to learn. But each explanation required compassion and understanding.

But right in there was the gift for us to learn.

Because Asperger's syndrome was in our lives, we had to learn to teach without judgment. We had to truly comprehend that behind every action, every word, and every intent was a reason, a belief, and a previously learned experience.

We had to learn to use our intuition and insight to understand why David reacted to certain environments or stimuli because the words he used often didn't explain the situation fully.

We had to seek to come to terms with that which was beyond face value. Through this, we gained enormous insight into human behavior and learned to constantly try to understand the reasons behind why people do what they do. These skills have been invaluable in our lives.

A SWOT ANALYSIS
OF DAVID

For the last nine years, I have studied and worked in the field of marketing. Prior to writing any marketing plan, the first step is a SWOT analysis, which helps you to identify the Strengths, Weaknesses, Opportunities, and Threats for any business. A SWOT analysis then gives you tools to create a plan for where you want to head.

When David moved to the technical college, the teachers asked me to write a report about him so they could get to know him on a personal level. The process of writing the report also helped us to understand David even more fully and helped the teachers to create strategies for him.

On reading this, I realized I had learned a lot about David during the time of writing it. It forced me to look at who he was, what he bought to the world, the challenges we faced, and the opportunities that could make life better for him.

Please feel free to use the criteria of this in helping you, or others, understand your child.

Who is David?

David is the eldest of three children with his two sisters, Alissa and Caitlin being both very high achievers and very independent. He has a soft and gentle personality and is very proud and very protective of his sisters. David and Alissa were best friends for many years, sleeping both in the same room until David was eleven. She was his teacher and his friend, and he relied on her to help him navigate the social world. He has had a great deal of trouble over the past couple of years coming to terms with the fact Alissa does not put him first anymore. He is still her greatest supporter and exceptionally proud of all her achievements.

David considers himself to be a second father to Caitlin, his youngest sister, and tries to be her advisor, her protector, and her mentor. He is very protective of her to the point of suffocation and gets very hurt when she doesn't respond in the way in which he expects.

David is very concerned about world issues such as world peace, poverty, and cruelty and sees those issues as being very important. He is also very aware of issues such as the Republic, the introduction of a GST [Goods and Services Tax]*, and social issues such as unemployment and crime.*

David loves "off the wall" humor such as The Goon Show, Monty Python, South Park, *and* The Simpsons. *He is also fascinated by science fiction,* Star Wars, *and anything to do with the planets and the stars.*

David's Strengths

David's strengths include acting—he has a photographic memory for memorizing lines, and he enjoys script writing and development. He has very little patience for people who cannot remember lines and sees that as an inherent weakness in their character! He sees Acting or the Arts as part of his future.

David has a photographic memory for anything of interest to him. He can tell stories about things he did at age three and four and yet cannot remember what he did yesterday. As a small child, David was able to count, spell, identify colors, and operate the computer by the age of three.

He is also exceptionally good at playing computer games and spends hours collecting and devising "cheats" for games. David receives many phone calls from his friends who ask him for ways to complete computer games. When he comes across a new game, he will stay on the computer or the Nintendo for hours until he can complete the game. This will often mean getting up in the middle of the night or rising early in the morning to get back to the game, long after we have told him to stop playing. Finishing the game becomes a total obsession for him.

David's Successes

David has had very few successes in his life mainly because he will stop doing something if he thinks he can't be perfect at it. He has received very few, if any, awards, at school, but when he does, his self-esteem is boosted incredibly. When he was in Year 8, he was awarded a certificate for Player of the Match for Volleyball, and he was so incredibly proud of that certificate—the glow lasted for two weeks.

David's Challenges

David likes things in his life to be orderly. If I tell David I will be home at 2:00 p.m. and I am late, he will be on the phone at 2:05, worrying about where I am. He dislikes sudden changes in routine and gets upset if things are not 100 percent clear to him. He is very sensitive to any disharmony in the house and needs to know everything is OK again before he can relax.

He dislikes people who are late, people who yell or are "mean" to him, or those who do not understand him. It does not worry him whether that person is a teacher, student, or person in power. If you get off on the wrong foot with David, then there is usually no hope for redemption!

David's greatest challenges surround being involved in a group or team activity and the effort required to stay focused on particular tasks either he perceives are difficult or involve abstract thinking and communication with others.

He finds focusing very difficult in class as many things bother him such as noise, heat and movement.

David is tired most of the day. Many Asperger's children are nocturnal and this is true for David. Although he is in bed most nights by 9:30, it is often past midnight before he finally settles down to sleep. He says he cannot stop his mind "thinking about things" to allow him to sleep. He wakes many times during the night, and this is especially noticeable when it is rainy or windy. We have tried many types of therapies to try to help him sleep, including relaxation, essential oils, bath before bed, and nothing seems to work in the long term. Consequently, we allow David to have at least a day off each fortnight, as we find it seems to help him recoup his energy.

Because of this tiredness and the challenges of his environment, David may react towards his peers in ways that are inappropriate. He finds it exceptionally difficult to respond to his peers spontaneously and so isolates himself because, in his words, "they all think I am a dork and I act like one." Hence, he does not attend any social activities outside of school with his peers.

David will usually not volunteer to be involved in team activities except Drama, although he does enjoy participation once he feels safe to be involved. He attends a Social Skills group on a Saturday morning with Department of Recreation and Sport and is one of the most enthusiastic players when playing soccer and basketball.

Support Needs

David requires:

1. Teacher aide support regularly and especially in the playground.

2. Simplification and breaking down of tasks required

3. An understanding that extra time may be required to complete assignments.

4. Modified exam procedures. David finds exam conditions extremely stressful and often has a mental block during exams.

5. Somebody who will encourage him to participate.

FOOD

Food can be a hot topic in the world of Asperger's children. Today there is much research available on the many types of food children react to. Many cases have proved that AS children benefit from diets in which some food groups are removed such as wheat, dairy, and sugar.

However, over the years, we tried many different ways in dealing with food intolerances. For many years, we restricted sugar (my children still remember the Easter I bought them carob Easter eggs, which they now liken to child cruelty). We also went through various phases of reducing wheat and dairy and watching food additives and preservatives.

The biggest issue we had at the time was that David's food likes included only a few items. He would eat as long as it was cereal, a certain type; apples, only Granny Smiths; vegetables, as long as it was carrots or potatoes; chicken; rice; and a certain type of ice cream. That was it! If we tried to introduce foods he didn't like, he would actually dry retch, and the food wouldn't get past his tongue. I haven't got room in this book to list the number of times I would buy expensive health or natural foods, spending what little money we didn't have on non-dairy, no wheat or sugar whatever, only to get it home to have David try it, then almost throw up. It became stressful to try to force him to eat certain foods, and some days it just wasn't worth the drama.

So we made a family decision to ensure we chose foods that were healthy and balanced across the food groups.

We reduced the amount of sugary food and convenience food in the house and made most of our own cakes and sweets. The children were seldom allowed to have soft drinks or cordials, and we limited the amount of take-out foods.

I can honestly say that, in our case, eliminating certain foods, other than sugar, red food coloring, and preservatives such as Flavor Enhancer 621 had little effect on him, although I can remember thinking numerous times that he wouldn't grow past a meter tall because he would never eat vegetables!

We made the decision to persist gently if we felt a certain food was causing issues, but the bottom line for us was everybody's sanity.

We ensure for the most part we buy fresh fruit and vegetables, cook and prepare most dinners at home, and are aware of hidden food additives and preservatives in all foods, including bread and cakes.

Today, David will try a variety of food, but basically he has a very bland diet. No frills like sauces or gravy, just a few plain, yet nourishing items he prefers. When he does have takeaway, it is always a Subway and he only drinks alcohol occasionally. But we have come a long way, and today he will attempt foods that years ago we could only dream about him eating.

NAVIGATING SCHOOLS

When we were searching for a school for David, we had very little choice available to us. Asperger's syndrome and the autism spectrum disorders were unknown during those days. We had little to work with and little understanding of special needs frameworks to fall back on. Thank goodness we found people, however, through the schools we chose, who took the initiative to not judge and to help us find programs for David that worked.

Most schools today have dedicated departments set aside with experienced learning support staff who are trained in working with students diagnosed with Asperger's syndrome. Seek these schools out. Ask questions about the programs schools run. Remember that, as this child's parent, you know him or her best. However, once your child gets to school, he or she is often a different person from the one you know at home. So be prepared to listen with an open mind and a compassionate heart.

After having worked in the education system, I have seen teachers who have their own agenda and expect children to fit into their rigid classroom rules. I have also seen parents who feel that their child is not achieving according to their expectations continually challenge and criticize teachers. Neither works.

Most of those who work in the learning support areas of a school are compassionate, caring teachers who truly value the best for your child. However, teachers are also under time restraints, educational expectations, and curricular guidelines. This is why it is important to create a strong partnership and an open dialogue between home and school.

We were so very lucky to have had Patty in our lives during David's early years. We were lucky because she is one of those unique individuals who truly do strive to understand each child individually. We spent time working together with her to develop strategies that we felt were right at the time. Sometimes they worked, sometimes they didn't, but we kept the dialogue open and continued to work within partnership.

Check in regularly with the learning support staff. If there are behavioral issues, look for the reason. It is essential for all to realize if your child with Asperger's is stressed, uncomfortable, unhappy, being bullied, being rejected, not understanding something, is too hot or too cold, or is too tired— or any variation of one or more of these —a behavioral issue will probably be the result.

Children with Asperger's syndrome react in inappropriate ways because in their minds, how they are being treated, or the situation they are in, is inappropriate.

But once you find the pattern, then you can set about creating the solutions.

DEBRIEFING TIME

Debriefing time for children with Asperger's is crucial and should be an essential part of their day.

Debriefing time can happen in a number of ways. For David, it was the ability to wander out of the classroom when things got too overwhelming for him. He had a certain spot he would go to, and he never wavered from that place. Every afternoon, as soon as he got home from school, he would walk around his favorite tree in the backyard, going over things in his head. It usually only took a few minutes or so, but once he had done that, he was fine—similar to an adult taking time out for a coffee break or shutting the door to have some quiet time.

Many people, educators included, have somehow gotten to a place where they believe those with Asperger's need to be kept on task. Yes, to some degree that's true, but we have found, through many years of experience, that if David was stressed in anyway, letting him stop what he was doing and letting him go out to wander and regroup was far better.

Ask your child's teacher, teacher's aide, or the head of the learning support department what debriefing strategies are available. Find a place where your child will feel safe and when it all becomes too much, let them go there. Set up the parameters and guidelines so they are clear on the time and the expectations – ten, fifteen, or twenty minutes in a "safe space" will save hours of debriefing later.

FRIENDS AND SOCIAL SKILLS

Making friends is probably the most challenging area for a child with Asperger's and especially for the parents who watch their child struggle with social nuances.

There have been many times in David's life where he has had a group of very good friends. In primary school, there were three boys who formed a bond with David. They were great friends, but as he grew older, the differences became very pronounced, especially through puberty. He just didn't understand their humor, their nonverbal cues, their music, and their need for other friends. David loved computer games and playing in the swimming pool, but that was about it. If conversations switched to something else, he was lost.

Most of David's friends also happened to be the sons of my friends. I am sure that many times these wonderful mothers took their sons aside and talked to them about David, helping the boys to understand why David did the things he did.

The teenage years were particularly tough, and we would often have to ask ourselves the question, "Are we dealing with puberty, or are we dealing with Asperger's?" The line was often very fine. In David's case, the Social Skills group was where he found his friends. Today, a number of the boys from Social Skills are still great friends, although they may only see each other once or twice a month.

David has made some acquaintances at university, but they only get together during his time at university, not as a general social group.

However, the interaction between David and his friends who have Asperger's is quite amazing to watch. We have often seen the boys sitting in the lounge or on the bean bags, game controllers in hand, playing an intense Nintendo game and chatting, with their eyes not moving from the screens (not unlike many males, I think). However, it is the conversations that take place that are very interesting.

Through the Social Skills groups, the boys have become accustomed to being very honest with each other. They have created a sacred space with confidentiality that goes along with being good friends. They don't talk about other people and they really don't care what goes on in other people's lives. They are actually a perfect example of what good friends are truly about.

The boys are exceptionally honest with each other. I have often heard them saying to another "Man, you are so autistic!" or "Stop being so obsessive." No judgments, just statements, then they get on with their life.

They understand differences; they acknowledge individuality and accept both those within each other. They don't care about what they wear. They don't care about whether they have the latest 'whatever'. To these boys, the relationship they have with each other is important in the moment.

If they have had enough of each other, they say so and it's OK to back off and walk away.

They are actually the model of a community in action: honest, individualistic, caring, and compassionate, without having to be part of a group. These are wonderful skills to have, and the world could do with more individuals who are willing to accept others without judgment.

SURVIVING OTHER PARENTS

A couple of years ago, a young mum at our school came and sat in my office in tears. She was walking her Asperger's child to the classroom when she walked into a conversation about her child. The other parents, standing with their backs to this woman, continued their conversation, not knowing she was there. They were discussing how they, as a group, were going to approach the teacher to make sure their children were not in her child's class. They also went on to talk about how they felt that she, as a parent, was obviously not disciplining her enough and that there were obviously problems at home.

She was devastated and I hugged her as she cried.

I remembered that feeling oh so well.

I have worked in schools for many years, and every year I see the same things occurring. Young mums standing outside the Kindergarten or Year 1 classrooms comparing reading levels, talking about teaching practices, discipline, and so on.

Young mums can be the cruelest people in the world, extremely judgmental and unforgiving in their beliefs about other parenting practices. Perhaps it's because we now have so much information at our fingertips. Perhaps because many women have stepped outside of the workforce and still trying to operate from a place of importance to find their sense of belonging.

Hence, these "power-yummy mummies" are often extremely critical of others, unkind in their remarks, and unsympathetic to those who don't have what they perceive as a "perfect" child, whatever that is!

For a parent of a child with Asperger's, this is a very unforgiving group to belong to. At this time, you need compassion and understanding, not judgment and criticism.

Try to not to get involved with this group, and seek out those who are compassionate in your own circle of friends. Where possible, help your child's teacher to truly understand your child and help the children in that class to also learn about Asperger's. Create relationships and support among the mothers of the children who are kind to your child (apples don't fall far from the tree!). The judgments may not stop, but by being able to talk to others about what you are going through helps you create your own support network that will be there for you in the tough times.

IT TAKES A VILLAGE TO RAISE A CHILD

Whenever I speak at different gatherings about David's Gift, I am simply overwhelmed by the amount of people who approach me later and say "My grandchild/ nephew/ niece or neighbor's child has just been diagnosed with Asperger's." Or "You know, everything you say describes my grandson/ granddaughter/niece/nephew." Grandparents and family members often observe differences that sometimes parents do not see and in many cases, can offer the most incredible support to the parents at times when life can be overwhelming.

When a child of difference enters the world, those affected are not only the parents and siblings but also, in many cases, the grandparents and the extended family.

Raising a child with Asperger's syndrome is tough. It is demanding both physically and emotionally, and there are times throughout this child's life, when the parents just cannot cope without the love and support of their friends and family.

At this time, parents of these children desperately need their own parents to talk to, to be hugged, to be understood, and to be able to express any emotion they need to, when it all becomes too much.

When my mother passed away, my father came to live with us for six months every year during the southern winters, and he was an amazing support. He never questioned or made judgments about what we were trying to do. He never criticized, nor did he challenge. He was incredibly patient and incredibly supportive of us.

I realize now that he, too, must have had questions about David and that, perhaps, he sometimes had his view about what we should or shouldn't be doing, but he never once raised those issues with us; he only ever gave us the most amazing support.

Whilst my sisters and their husbands, my brother and his wife all lived in different states, whenever we did get together they accepted, and did their best to understand, the intricate nature of Asperger's, often asking questions about how to interact with David and helped to support us.

Many times during this process, we, as parents, need to revert to our child place again, a time when we need to hang up the parent hat and put on the child hat; to be able to sit with our own parents or siblings and to be able to simply pour out our hearts.

It is not a time of judgment, nor do you need to do anything. But it is a time when you need to be there for your own child, brother or sister and allow them to grieve, cry, laugh, explore, question, challenge, rage, or vent.

A grandparent or older person's role in helping raise a child with Asperger's is crucial. An older person often brings with them patience and understanding, and can help out in so many ways in order to give the parents the opportunity to take some much needed time out.

I have often heard the statement 'It takes a village to raise a child' this is certainly true with Asperger's syndrome. I can't emphasize strongly enough how grandparents and family members can be the most incredible support during this time.

THOSE WHO HAVE BEEN THERE

There are so many people to thank for this journey, so many people who have been stalwart friends, positive educators, great hand holders, shoulders for crying on and wine buddies. Thank you for being such a part of this journey:

Our ever supportive family—my father, Cal Johnston, and family members Jo Johnston, Jeannine Johnston, Martin and Chris Johnston, Michaela Johnston, Ken Hardie, Aaron and Patrick, Brad and Katie, Eleanore and Harry, Jack and Tess; our extended family—Mary and Jim Slingsby and all the Slingsbys; Paul, Ben, Luke, Anna, and Matty Eves, our family in Canada—Judy and Ted Benedict; the Owen clan; the Johnston clan; Patty Lloyd, David's junior school teachers and friends; David's senior school teachers; all those at Gold Coast Technical and Further Education institute and Griffith University Disability Services who went out of their way to help; the Coomera clan—Jan, Kirsty and Daniel Sorrensen; Donna, Steve, Katie, Emma, and Sarah Champness; Bronwyn, Des, Jake, Caitlin, and Maddie Lacy; Paula Axford-Wood; the fabulous luncheon three, who make us a foursome—Anne Anderson, Jenny Jones, and Liz Thomson; and the always amazing Gold Coast Recreation and Sport people. Those involved in the book production: Iain and

Lou McGregor and the crew at P's in a Pod, who are not only awesome designers but also great friends; Web designer Dale Napier, Mark Burgin, for the wonderful photography; and the wonderful book PR whiz Chelsea McLean.

But most of all to my family: Gerry, my best friend, soul mate, confidante, and the best cook in the whole world; Alissa and Caitlin, absolutely shining lights whose very presence on this planet make it a better place to be; and, finally, to David, whose gift to us all, makes this incredible life something worth writing about. How lucky I am you chose me to be your mother!

ABOUT THE AUTHOR

Sally THIBAULT *Dip. Prof. Counseling, ADAPEF*

In 1979, Sally commenced a career as a fitness instructor in Canada, a career she enjoyed for over fifteen years. During that time, she developed Aerobic Instructor Training courses, training over four hundred aerobics instructors; hosted Canada's first Cable TV fitness show; and facilitated the world's largest indoor aerobics class with two thousand participants in Edmonton, Alberta, Canada, in 1982.

After returning to Australia with her husband, Sally developed seminars and keynote presentations on "The Art of Losing Weight Permanently and Surviving Stress."

During this time, their oldest child David was diagnosed with Asperger's syndrome, which resulted in a change in direction for her family.

In 2000, she began a new career as the Director of Community Relations for a Queensland Independent school, a position she held for ten years. During that time, she served as the Vice President of ADAPE Queensland (Association of Development Professionals in Education (ADAPE) from 2004 through 2008 and presented at three ADAPE International Conferences in Perth 2004, Auckland 2006, and Queensland 2008 on the topics of Educational Marketing and was awarded the honor of 'Fellow' for service to the Association.

She holds a Diploma of Professional Counseling, and is a member of the Board of Trustees of *The Goda Foundation*; a private educational foundation offering global education and leadership experiences for students.

Sally lives in Queensland Australia with her husband Gerry and their three children.

SPEAKING ENGAGMENTS

Sally is a sought after speaker and gifted teacher, specializing in the areas of Asperger's syndrome, Parenting teenagers, and Self-leadership. She also facilitates regular in-service days for counselors, specialists, teachers and support staff and runs regular seminars and webinars on topics related to Asperger's syndrome and the effect on family dynamics.

To book Sally for speaking engagements visit www.davidsgift.com, or email sallythibault@gmail.

You can also join in the conversation at Facebook www.facebook.com/aspergersparentconnect

Or follow Sally on twitter @SallyThibault

A FREE GIFT FOR PARENTS

Please visit the Web site (www.davidsgift.com/free-school-report) to download the *Free School Report*. This report, in template format, is for school professionals, teachers and all other people in the education system who may be dealing with your child. This information may help them to discover strategies to make your child's experience at school more rewarding and less stressful. The template takes you through a step-by-step method to customize your report with your child's details. Sally has brought her experience with the school system into this report as a guide for parents to help maximize their child's experience while at school.

OTHER BOOKS BY SALLY THIBAULT

ASPERGER'S, BULLYING AND SCHOOLS, How to make your Child Bully-Resilient at School and for Life

Children diagnosed with Asperger's are 80% more likely to be bullied at school than any other group of children. In her new book, Sally draws on her experience as a Professional Counselor, parent and her 10 year experience working in the school system, with a powerful, practical new book designed to help parents teach their ASD child bully-resilient strategies for school and for life.

www.aspergersandbullying.com

WISE MOTHERS – Parenting Teenagers in the Facebook Era

The story of one woman's search for wisdom. Wise Mothers, Parenting Teenagers in the Facebook Era, examines the impact of technology, media and social media on the relationship between mothers and daughters and the urgent need for wisdom in parenting teenage girls.

Available from www.davidsgift.com.au

37462771R00152

Made in the USA
Lexington, KY
03 December 2014